Praise for

REID THOMPSON &

the
Unicorn
Frequency

"Exhilarating. Braiding together life and energetic principles, *The Unicorn Frequency* is the new contemporary guide to the law of attraction. R.T. speaks in a way that makes you feel as though you are sipping a Moroccan mint tea with a life-long friend overlooking a brilliant ocean sunrise. The easy stylings, relatable life-happenings, and levity creates a breezy space of remembering who we all are with the universe. A must read that is refreshing and practical, with a kiss of *Hello, Dolly!*"

—Stefan T.Wong, Attorney, Harvard-Certified Strategist,

and Author of *Talking to Crows*

"Reid is a brilliant intuitive and masterful with his work. He is able to translate vibrations from your Inner Being, guiding you back home to you. His brilliance of integrating practices and study of the Law of Attraction leaves you feeling inspired and having much clarity and direction for next steps with whatever you are focusing on. I have loved working with Reid the past year and would HIGHLY recommend him as your guide."

—Ashley W.

"Reid is a gifted guide who helped me understand the importance of tuning to my real preferences in any situation, but perhaps the most natural gift he has is transferring his understanding of the goodness of each one of us simply by being in his presence.

This was a life changing experience for me that I will forever be grateful for. I love sessions with him."

—Mandee S.

"I have had multiple sessions with Reid and I will continue to meet with him because when I sit with Reid, I feel incredibly safe and seen.

One of the things I enjoy the most is how I feel he truly sees my inner being, and senses my potential and what is ready for me in my vortex.

I always feel like I can engage in my life, my marriage, my motherhood and my work from a more centered place after having a session with him. He is truly gifted in guiding and soothing. Thank you, Reid."

—Heather C.

"Reid is a fabulous guide.

His wisdom and understanding of divine guidance is impeccable.

I have expanded my own comfort around my preferences through Reid's presence. That might seem odd to need to be comforted around following your own preferences but it is true!

We are so often conditioned to know about others that we loose sight of our own selves.

I am forever expanded because of Reid."

—Liz Hays

the Unicorn
Frequency

the Unicorn
Frequency

**UNLEASH THE
MAGIC OF MORE MONEY,
MORE FREEDOM & MORE FUN**

REID THOMPSON

Published by
MANDALA
TREE PRESS
mandalatreepress.com

Paperback ISBN: 9781954801813
Hardcover with Dust Jacket ISBN: 9781954801820
Case Laminate Hardcover ISBN: 9781954801837
eBook ISBN: 9781954801844

SEL027000 SELF-HELP / Personal Growth / Success
SEL032000 SELF-HELP / Spiritual
OCC019000 BODY, MIND & SPIRIT / Inspiration & Personal Growth

Cover design by Reid Thompson and Kaitlin Barwick
Typesetting by Kaitlin Barwick
Edited by Justin Greer and Valene Wood

theunicornfrequency.com
reidthompsoncreative.com
reidintheworld.com

I dedicate this book with love and appreciation
to my sweet daughters, Katie and Mary.

I love you.

Contents

More money. More freedom. More fun.
When you're a unicorn, you expect MORE.
More travel, more opportunities, more access,
more wonder, more thrill.
MORE MAGIC.

I openly admit that I am a unicorn. But I'm not the only one.
There are others. You could be one too, if you knew how to
tune out everyone else and their opinions. If instead
you were immersed in the fullness of YOU.

In this book, I will show you how
I did it—and how you can too.

Chapter 1

MY UNICORN ORIGIN STORY

MY LIFE HASN'T ALWAYS BEEN MAGICAL. LIKE SO MANY OF US, I had been guiding myself through life using a compass of reason. The results were moderately successful. I was a divorced dad with two beautiful daughters from a previous marriage to a woman. I was a successful creative director for a fortune 500 company. And I was finally embracing my authentic self as a gay man after decades of feeling trapped by my religious upbringing. Life was good. But it wasn't as thrilling as what I am currently living. This book takes you on my journey of making decisions in a completely new way. I replaced my old compass of reason with a completely new north star that measures each decision through a filter of "fun energy."

I discovered this new approach while at a seminar. This pursuit of fun is what led me to the realization that we each have the ability to be unicorns. Unicorns are considered "rare," but this magic is available to all of us. Rare things happen for me because I've come to *expect* the rare as my new normal. We have been told or assume it is only for the lucky ones, but I will show you how to unlock the unicorn inside you. You simply have to connect to what I am calling the unicorn frequency. Just like a radio station, in order to receive its broadcast, you have to tune to its specific frequency.

Frequency?

Think of it this way. When you walk into a room and someone you care about is mad at you and not talking to you, *that* is a frequency of energy that you easily feel. You have immediately tuned in to it. No one has to speak it or write it down or spell it out. You intuitively feel it because you easily sense the energy of this frequency.

If you were with your best friend and they suddenly started laughing uncontrollably, you would easily and naturally join them in their frequency of joy. It's contagious. There are as many frequencies as there are emotions; some of them are positive and some negative. What if you were more alert to and therefore very deliberate about the frequencies you allowed yourself to join? I can tell you from personal experience that your life would dramatically transform.

The Unicorn Frequency Dances with the Frequency of Fun

I started with fun, and this embodiment of fun grew until I realized I was in unicorn territory. A unicorn is filled up on the inside with fun. Once you enter this kingdom of fun, you will meet many happy people and creatures frolicking about. When you scan the horizon, you will notice an opulent castle on the hill. There is a magnificent entrance constructed entirely out of rainbows (duh) where the unicorns live a life of freedom and abundance and non-stop magic. This book is not only about how to find this kingdom of fun, but how to actually move into that castle on the hill: into your full unicorn status.

To be a unicorn, you have to start doing things differently than the rest of the world. The magic of your own dreams and preferences are yours alone to cultivate and celebrate. You have a unicorn frequency within you. But since you grew up caring so much about what others think about you and your choices, you end up living most of your life in a frequency of split energy. To be a unicorn you have to fully own the beauty and magic of you. A unicorn does not spend time measuring and evaluating how they stack up when compared to the others around them. They know they are amazing—and its full steam ahead!

So really, we are all unicorns. Each of us has magic and brilliance within us. But that frequency or reality is not accessible from lower frequencies of hate, lack, fear, self-doubt, etc. You access the magic and brilliance of a unicorn through a diet of joy and fun. This diet is pure love of joy and fun and love for *yourself*, a love for your fellow humans, and a love for this beautiful world.

How Do I Go from Normal to Unicorn?

The unicorn frequency is similar to a WIFI signal that is always available and always broadcasting. But you'll need the password—and that password is F-U-N.

Fun is the rainbow bridge to a thrilling life. Fun is one of the highest frequencies because it includes no resistance. When you are engaged in the act of fun, you have no split energy. You are not including serious problems that you are distracted to solve. You are in pure energy flow, and that, my friends, is the receiving mode. That is the key that lets in everything that thrills you. Before you know it, you'll look around and have the life of a unicorn. It won't feel like one single poof where everything is suddenly different. Your life will transform one step at a time. It will feel logical, incremental, bold, brave, and even terrifying at times as you release old belief systems that you thought kept you safe but, in fact, held you back. When you are evaluating yourself based on how everyone else defines "life," you are not in your truth. When you are not grounded in your truth, you don't feel the stability of your safety. Because a unicorn always feels safe, they are in the act of fun. They are in a never-ending loop of magic. They are in a never-ending loop of appreciation and love for themselves.

Your Expectation Governs Your Universe

Why is this unicorn frequency so life changing for us as humans? It's so much simpler than I ever imagined. I've discovered it boils down to the transforming power of expectation. I've learned through life experience that you can't receive beyond what you expect (what you believe is possible) *or* what you feel you deserve.

Your expectation is your reality. If you expect the meeting at work to be painfully boring and unproductive, it always is. If you expect to decline in health as you age—guess what? You will. If you understand that you are magical and then expect your day to be magical, it will be. When I mastered feeling magical on the inside, my exterior world reflected that magic back to me. Expectation unlocks everything.

When I started applying the expectation of experiencing my life as if I were a unicorn, my ability to imagine more for myself exploded exponentially.

Learning from the Best: My Unicorn Mentors

I am a huge advocate of personal growth and therefore leveraging the benefits of working with a personal coach. To say that I have benefitted from working with a coach would be a massive understatement. I have grown lightyears due to this one-on-one transfer of knowledge. But I had never considered working with a mentor or coach until I actually met one.

My first coach was a woman I met at my second law of attraction seminar named KT Brady. I first spotted her seated a few rows in front of me. Looking back, it's funny that I had such clarity that I wanted to know her when I could mostly just see the back of her head. Knowing what I know today, it makes sense that I could easily, naturally feel powerful resonance inside my body that she was going to be important to my desire to know more about how the universe works and how I fit into everything. My intention to expand my awareness created the path for us to meet. She was a cooperative component to my powerful desire. I decided to introduce myself to her during a break. I had no idea she was a life coach when I saw her sitting in front of me. After meeting her and having a chance to get to know her a little, everything inside me was screaming, *I want to know what she knows!* If she isn't a high priestess unicorn, I don't know who is.

KT and I started with one-off sessions which soon grew into a twice weekly program of sessions that lasted an entire twelve months. The trajectory of my life changed astronomically from this work. My eternal journey is forever expanded. It was my desire and intention to be the fullest version of myself that gave me the clarity and the emotional green light to partner with a coach and leverage this way of working that I had not yet experienced. I followed my own inner guidance and said yes to myself in a very powerful and transformative way when I started working with her.

At the end of our twelve months together she paid me the biggest compliment. She told me that I was not "one in a million but one in a billion" because of my willingness to hear my guidance that came through during our sessions and then act on it immediately. To trust and follow my guidance was what made me so rare in her eyes. That was thrilling feedback to hear from someone I respect and hold in such high regard.

The Role of Expectation

It was my second coach, Liz Hays, that introduced me to this unicorn language and its applications to my life. This expanded practice of expectation started with a conversation about the things I desired being delivered to me by my inner being and the universe in ways that would knock my socks off. I loved how that phrase of "knock my socks off" felt as she said it. I could feel how my expectation was higher with that phrase than with any other language. I started using it in my morning meditation or alignment work. For example, I would say to my inner being, "Blow my socks off with how much of my dreams I can experience today." Another example was, "Blow my socks off with how good I can feel today."

Then one day Liz started using unicorn language. She was about to attend an event and texted me, "How does this scenario play out for a unicorn?" Liz was applying this to a normal, everyday scenario. I felt the thrill and brilliance of framing everything within that question. I could powerfully sense how different my expectation felt when guided by this type of unicorn framework. So, I started working with this unicorn language daily. Another day or two later, in her role as my coach, she texted me this beautiful suggestion: Ask your divine team, "I want to see and sense how I am a magical unicorn manifestor of money." I loved how this felt as I read it. I began customizing this to apply to whatever topic I was focused on each day. "I want to see how I am a magical unicorn manifestor of a deep, romantic relationship." "I want to see how I am a magical unicorn manifestor of luxury travel." "I want to see how I am a magical unicorn manifestor of ease and thrill and clarity." My focus continued along these lines every day. I could feel inside me the enormous difference in my level of expectation when I shifted my ability to "think big" as a human to this new lens of what a unicorn would expect. The difference in energy was astonishing. As expressed earlier, we can't manifest beyond what we believe is possible. We can't manifest beyond what we expect. We also can't manifest something we don't believe we deserve or are worthy to receive.

The Role of Worthiness

Let's discuss this topic of worthiness. You don't have to earn your worthiness. You came to this life worthy and deserving of maximum abundance, joy, freedom, and health. Anything wonderful you desire; you are worthy of receiving. Understanding your worthiness allows you to love yourself, always. It's about loving yourself now, exactly where you are, on your path *today*. Loving yourself when you accomplish wonderful things and loving yourself equally when you make a mistake. And this extends to loving others. Everyone is on their own path and their own timetable. Don't make others wrong for where they are today. You don't have to join them if it doesn't thrill you. But letting them be ok where they are is liberating. The freedom to be you is the same frequency that allows everyone else to freely be them. When you judge someone else as being wrong or living a life that is wrong, you are focused in negative energy. You are not inhabiting the frequency of the beauty and wholeness of your highest self.

It is logical that a unicorn is creating magic from a place of knowing their self-worth. So, the more I opened up my expectation for what was possible for me, coupled with the absolute knowing that I deserved it, the more it came true for me. And I wasn't sitting passively by, waiting and hoping for cool things. I was asking myself, "What thrills me? What would I like to do next? Where would I love to live? What kind of emotions would I like to feel in a romantic relationship?"

What would be *fun* to do right now?

It All Started with FUN

Contrary to how we've been raised, it's not through blood, sweat, and tears that we accomplish our dreams, but through playful, lighthearted energy. This might sound counterintuitive, but in reality, there's nothing *more* intuitive to the core of our being than having F-U-N. It's the number one reason we came forth: to play. Fun is a pathway to transformation. Yes, fun!

Notice how small children are on a never-ending quest to have fun. They are pure and unspoiled by the cares of the world. Like unicorns, they aren't stressed about paying bills like the adults. Left to their own devices, they spring out of bed to start playing. As they grow, they are educated to take on more and more responsibility.

But what if our first "responsibility" or focus or priority was to *feel* the energy of creativity, fun, and play?! And what if our second priority was to tend to our "to do" list? How would that change our lives?

This question was how it all started. I was attending my first Abraham Hicks seminar on the law of attraction. In the closing remarks, I heard two ideas that completely blew my mind:

1. Life is supposed to be fun. You spend too much time in the cares of the world and on your grocery list and errands and work responsibilities.
2. If you focus on having fun, life's problems will take care of themselves.

As I took in these statements, I immediately recognized them as true. I knew from the core of my being that if I applied these ideas to my life, they would not only transform my life, but result in financial freedom as well!

So, I set out on a twelve-month "science" experiment to apply these ideas and document what I learned along the way. I intended to prove that the deliberate practice of tuning to all things fun is an astonishing, counterintuitive path to financial abundance. Hearing these words is one thing but experiencing them is another. What about money? What about all the other facets of my life that needed to be taken care of? The balls of countless responsibilities I had to keep in the air? I couldn't just set all that down in the name of having a good time, could I? I decided I had to find out.

My "science" experiment was this: when faced with a choice, I'd ask myself, "Of the options in front of me, what sounds the most fun? What do I have the most enthusiasm for?" Then I'd chase the fun, regardless of what my lifelong pattern of "common sense" might have historically guided me to do. At the beginning it was as simple as "I have thirty minutes before my first meeting . . . what would feel fun to do with that time?" Sometimes the answer would be to go to my favorite coffee shop and savor a latte. I didn't abandon my then-reality and drive off a cliff or quit my job. I started with an intention of per-meating fun into as many moments of my life as I could think of. My first concept of infusing maximum fun into my life was planning more travel where I could. For example, of the travel ideas in front of me, which one do I have the most enthusiasm for? Almost always, there was a clear winner.

Trusting My New Compass

I would soon learn that I could trust that enthusiastic feeling inside me. I could isolate that feeling that was vibrating inside me *and* I could trust it. Once I had recognized that feeling, it became more pronounced and easier to tune in to. It became my companion and my new navigational device. My North Star and compass. This new guid-ance system radically changed how I made decisions. It replaced my decision-making process. Instead of looking from a filter of scarcity or lack to decide if I could do something, I made decisions based on my filter of enthusiasm. This has changed my life. And I know for a fact that it can change yours too.

The Frequency of Abundance

That feeling of enthusiasm (or fun or joy or exhilaration or love) is the life force that animates the universe. When we are flowing in those feelings, we are flowing *in* and *with* the abundance of the universe. In fact, those feelings *are* the very energy of abundance. The same energy that animates the universe in well-being. So, when we have decided on, sought out, and tuned in to that energy, we are not separate from abundance. We are at one with abundance. We *are* the energy of abundance. Tell me, how does abundance *not* show up in your life when you have accomplished the alignment to this energy?

Alignment to this energy of the highest vibration is a choice. You can all too easily choose to calibrate to the drama going down in the break room at work. Or you can deliberately choose to calibrate to the frequency that draws abundance to you. There are many, many realities going on in the same moment. Many perspectives one can choose. Glass half full and glass half empty. It's not that one is true, and one is false. Both are true. But you can only focus on one in any given moment. Which you choose as your focus determines your reality.

Before and After

Here are some highlights of the "before and after" of my life following the completion of my first twelve months of this experiment:

- I'm no longer working. Full stop. That is radical change. Instead of turning in timesheets, I now wake up when I want, and do what I want when I want. This alone blows my mind on a regular basis.

- I'm now an entrepreneur who follows his "yes energy" when deciding what projects I want to pursue. I now live in a confidence that these business opportunities will present themselves in the perfect timing. One already has. Before, I was terrified of leaving my corporate security blanket, but now I'm letting the universe yield to me as I need it. That's a radical releasing of old belief systems. That's shifting the source of my security from conditions outside of me to where it belongs . . . ME! I *am* the abundance, not my employer.

- I'm single. My willingness to acknowledge the clarity of my preferences and then my willingness to follow the calling to feel better by leaving my relationship has transformed me and my reality. I realized that I love the solitude of living on my own with no other energy interrupting my flow. For now, that is my truth.

- I'm headed to Greece using a one-way plane ticket and will spend four months hopping from one hotel to another. My only plan is to have fun and be spontaneous. My most extravagant vacation before this was a three-week vacation each year. Now I'm not on vacation, it's just my normal daily life.

I'm not bragging. I'm stating my new reality. If someone had told me before I started this experiment that this would be my life, I would have screamed, "How!? Please tell me how."

None of this is technically hard. It's simply counterintuitive to why, what, and *how* we've lived so far. It's counterintuitive to how we've been taught to accomplish our dreams.

Chapter 2

UNICORN SCHOOL

IN CASE SOME OF THE TERMINOLOGY I'VE USED IS NEW TO YOU, I thought I'd pause and explain some of the most important ideas and terms that have been the foundation for my unicorn transformation as I've applied this filter of fun.

I didn't understand every term being used as I read new books and watched hours of Abraham YouTube videos, but I was amazed at how everything I heard made perfect sense. Following the terms are concepts that are equally foundational and worth taking the time to understand. As one of my coaches said, sometimes we slow down so we can then go fast.

Inner Being

As humans, we have dimension. We are not one dimensional. Interestingly, the word dimension means two measures: "di" means apart and "mension" means measure. There are two distinct measures of us. We have all heard the expression "body and soul." You could say that the first measure is the part of us that is nonphysical or the "soul" part of us and the second measure is the physical part of us. We are energy that is both physically focused and nonphysically focused in this human experience.

Point of Attraction

You are a vibrational being and at all times are broadcasting the frequency of whatever emotion you are feeling in each moment. This is your point of attraction that the universe is responding to, that the law of attraction is responding to.

Vortex

Vortex is the term that represents a person's hopes and dreams all being recorded, captured, and held in a "vibrational escrow" or savings account. All of it is real and ready to move from the nonphysical thinking or vibrational realm to the manifested physical realm where you can feel it, touch it, hear it, smell it, taste it. Every single thing that exists has to be thought of first before it can manifest into its physical form. Your vortex is your collection of wildest dreams and deepest held desires. Whenever you've had a difficult relationship, your ideal relationship was launched into this vortex that we each include. There is a book devoted exclusively to the explanation of this concept written by Esther and Jerry Hicks. When we become a vibrational match to what is in our vortex, amazing things unfold— and it is unmistakable to us when this happens. I have experienced the recognition of these vortex desires manifesting into my physical experience and it is thrilling.

Law of Attraction 101

We are energy. Everything is energy. There is actual science behind this idea of FUN.

One of the laws of the universe is gravity. Another, lesser-discussed law that governs the universe and orders our lives is called "the law of attraction." This law explains that everything is energy, and each frequency of energy attracts to it the same frequency. Like attracts like . . . hence the law of attraction.

We are energetic, vibrational beings. Our emotions determine the frequency of our energy. Depression is a low, slow frequency. A high emotion, such as love, appreciation, gratitude, and joy, is an example of a fast, high frequency. Whichever frequency we are at attracts people, experiences, and conditions that are of a similar frequency. You could also say that we attract a "vibrational match" to whichever frequency we are at. Think of the old saying "birds of a feather flock together."

We all learned in our earliest science classes that the basic building block of matter is the atom. "Each individual atom consists of smaller particles—namely, electrons and nuclei. These particles are electrically charged, and the electric forces on the charge are responsible for holding the atom together."[1]

Stay with me. These nuggets from science help make sense of what many quickly dismiss as spiritual, faith-based, or metaphysical theories. So, let's ground ourselves in some basics about matter as energy.

- All matter is composed of very small particles, which can exist independently.
- Particles of matter are continuously moving.
- Particles of matter attract each other.[2]

Some medical practices we accept as normal are entirely based on our bodies as energy. For example, an EKG measures the energy of the heart. An EEG measures electrical activity in the brain. Brain cells communicate via electrical impulses and are active all the time (even as we sleep). We are energy!

Vibration and Frequency

The energy of your emotional state determines what you are attracting into your experience. Every subject has a vibrational charge. When you focus on any topic, you are in essence tuning in to that topic's vibrational frequency. Whatever you focus upon, you attract to yourself. Therefore, whether you focus on a negative or positive subject, you amplify the vibrational essence of that subject and attract more of it to you. Let's say you enter a conversation where someone is complaining about shitty behavior from a spouse or boss. In a matter of seconds, others will join in and share their similar stories as well. The energy of "shitty behavior" gains momentum and more stories about that behavior continue to grow. That's the law of attraction.

But you can see the same dynamic at work on positive experiences or subjects too. Someone could be sharing examples of adorable things their child has said and you naturally find and share your own favorite adorable story. We are doing this without realizing it. Once we understand how it works, we can radically transform our lives by deliberately choosing what we focus on. When you intentionally focus on the things that are going right in your life, you will start to notice more things that are positive in their essence and are now easier to find. The positive is showing up because you are focused on it. Whatever you focus on grows. Like attracts like. This is what is called the law of attraction.

All Roads Eventually Lead to Oprah

I can definitely attribute my transformed life to learning and applying the law of attraction. My path to understanding life in this new way was incremental. One bread crumb leading to another. I didn't realize that was what was happening at the time, but I love looking back and seeing that my inner being, my higher self, was calling me closer. The breadcrumbs on my path to discovering the law of attraction came to me through a series of books. I love the expression "when the student is ready, the teacher emerges."

For years I had been consumed in the cycle of negative news. While "doom scrolling" through the reporting of the storming of the U.S. Capitol Building, I noticed a tweet that caught my attention. The tweet said, "My 5-year-old grandson just nonchalantly asked me why the man in the hallway is watching us. I live alone!"[3] That thread was full of stories where children could see loved ones that had just passed away because they were not yet educated to believe otherwise. Someone in the thread included a reference to a book about reincarnation. For some reason this spoke to me, so I downloaded it and started reading. This book blew my mind and opened me up to new concepts around reincarnation, vibration, and even the idea that we all have an "inner being" or "higher self."

A few weeks later, if I'm remembering correctly, I was entertaining myself on YouTube and I was served up an Oprah video where she recommended two books. Oprah delivered this recommendation with such fervor that I could feel undeniable desire within me. Knowing what I know today, it clearly was my nonphysical inner being that was filling me with absolute resonance for the book I was about to read. Both books sounded ground-breaking: *A New Earth* by Eckhart Tolle and *The Law of Attraction* by Esther and Jerry Hicks. Below the Oprah book episode, I saw an hour-and-seventeen-minute interview that Oprah conducted with Esther and Jerry.[4] After watching the thorough, fascinating interview, I knew that this was the next book I wanted to read.

Here's the Amazon summary I found as I purchased my digital copy for my Kindle:

> This book presents the powerful basics of the original Teachings of Abraham. Within these pages, you'll learn how all things, wanted and unwanted, are brought to you by this most powerful law of the universe, the law of attraction. (That which is like unto itself is drawn). [This] has been alluded to by some of the greatest teachers in history, it has never before been explained in as clear and practical terms as in this latest book by *New York Times* best-selling authors, Esther and Jerry Hicks.[5]

Jerry and Esther Hicks

As I mentioned earlier, Jerry and Esther Hicks explain that just as the law of gravity is at work in our universe, the law of attraction is also a law of physics ordering the universe based on the idea that "like attracts like." You attract what you think about whether you want it or not.

I think it's important for my readers to hear how Esther Hicks has explained what "Abraham" is all about. It's not the easiest phenomenon to articulate and I want my readers to see how Esther explains all of this herself and undoubtedly how Abraham articulates their role and purpose. Here's what is posted on the Abraham-Hicks website under the tab "About Us."

> . . . who, or what, is/are, Abraham . . . really?
>
> To Dr. Wayne Dyer they are "the great Masters of the Universe!"

A veritable who's-who of authors, speakers and teachers continue to publicly acknowledge and praise the immense value of the wisdom that is pouring forth through Esther.

Abraham has described themselves as "a group consciousness from the nonphysical dimension"

"Jerry and Esther never used the word channeling," Abraham reflects. "It is used when applied to them, but they have never used it, because it means many things of which they are not . . ."

"You could leave the channeling out of it. Call it inspiration; that's all it is. You don't call the basketball player a channeler, but he is; he's an extension of Source Energy. He's channeling the broader essence of who he is into the specifics of what he is about."

Esther herself calls Abraham "infinite intelligence."

We say check out Abraham for yourself. If watching or listening or reading the words of Abraham feels good to you, then you're in the right place. If they sound "off" to you, or maybe even a little bit annoying—adventure on![6]

Consuming the Book

So, now that I had the book, I dove into it immediately. Everything I read was a revelation yet logical. Everything I'd lived and studied over the course of my life felt as if it was culminating in this account of how the universe is ordered. How *we* are ordered. Since then, I've attended twelve law of attraction seminars taught by Esther Hicks herself. I've read many books and consumed hundreds (maybe thousands?) of hours of workshop discussions from other seminars dating back thirty years. I've also worked with two coaches that I met at these seminars. The personalized coaching I received was the biggest game changer for me.

Ms. Hicks says often that "words don't teach, life experience teaches." That rings true with what I have lived. Having grown up in an organized religion and having left that religion, I personally am not interested in anything that is promised by another human expert that I can't apply and prove for myself. I am open to new ideas, but I am no longer interested in taking someone else's word for anything. I need to prove everything for myself. Or I need to have lived something that tells me that what they are saying is true for me too. I'm not against those who love their religion or faith. In fact, I personally celebrate *not* being against anything. I'm simply sharing what appealed to me about the ideas I read in the book and heard in the videos and seminars I've attended.

Wanted and Unwanted

Another profound idea that changed how I looked at my life was the idea that "in every particle of the universe, there is wanted and unwanted." This idea blew my mind and yet was so logical. I wasn't being asked to deny that bad things are happening or aren't true. Bad things are in fact happening. But good things are happening as well. Which do you want to expand in your life: pleasant or unpleasant? Wanted or unwanted? Which do you want to be most aware of? Which feels better? The better you feel, the higher your frequency. The higher your frequency, the more you are a vibrational match to health, to abundance, to joy. Like attracts like.

When you go to a buffet, there are foods you like and foods that disgust you. You logically choose only the foods you love. No one is claiming the foods you don't like aren't there. They definitely are there! But you know that you're not obligated to pick those. It would never occur to you to say, "I demand you remove all the foods I don't like." You just scan your options and choose what you like. Please apply this idea to the topics in your daily life you choose to focus your attention on. Which thoughts do you allow yourself to entertain and continue with? If it doesn't feel good, abandon it. Focus instead on what feels fun, what feels life-affirming. This improves your life. There is always good and bad, positive and negative, right in front of us in life's moment-by-moment buffet. Choose wisely. Choose on purpose.

Life Is a Radio Station

If you notice someone's annoying habits, your awareness of annoying things grows. If you focus upon the pleasing qualities of someone or something, your awareness for pleasing things grows. The law of attraction isn't judging right or wrong, deserving or undeserving; it simply is an amplifier of that which your thought or attention is focused upon or tuned to.

When you tune your radio to a country music station, that's what you expect to hear playing, that's what you expect to find: country music. You wouldn't complain, "I wish they'd play classical music." It would be ridiculous to think, "Life isn't fair. I never hear my favorite classical songs on this station." You would intentionally tune to the station that plays the music you do love. As in the food buffet example, you wouldn't ask the radio stations to remove all music except the music you like. You know your job is to find the music you like by scanning for it and tuning to it.

Notes

1. James Trefil, Sharon Bertsch McGrayne, and George F. Bertsch, "atom," *Encyclopedia Britannica*, 2 Jul. 2023, https://www.britannica.com/science/atom.

2. anshitaagarwal1609, "Matter is Made of Tiny Particles," *Geeks for Geeks*, 21 Jul. 2021, https://www.geeksforgeeks.org/matter-is-made-of-tiny-particles/.

3. Sassy Nanna @MelisaGillet, *Twitter*, 19 Feb. 2021.

4. Manifest Reality, "Oprah Esther Abraham Hicks Interview Law of Attraction The Secret," *YouTube*, 29 Nov. 2018, https://www.youtube.com/watch?v=P--lYlMgv6Q.

5. Esther and Jerry Hicks, "The Law of Attraction: The Basics of Teachings of Abraham," *Amazon Prime*, accessed Oct. 2023, https://www.amazon.com/Law-Attraction-Basics-Teachings-Abraham/dp/1401917593.

6. "About Abraham-Hicks," *Abraham-Hicks Publications*, accessed Oct. 2023, https://www.abraham-hicks.com/about/.

Chapter 3

UNICORN WISDOM

LET'S GO A LITTLE DEEPER. IN THIS SECTION I GO INTO MORE detail and apply some of my own life experiences to additional core concepts that are essential to living a life beyond your wildest dreams.

Take Other People Out of Your Equation

Everyone has their own inner being, so stop worrying about other people. Stop trying to be someone else's inner being. Everyone comes with their own internal guidance, their own connection to Source Energy. We *are* Source Energy. When we take on the responsibility of being someone else's "solution" or fixing their life for them, we are out of alignment. We are working from a false premise. First of all, no one needs to be fixed. Yes, people have challenges and difficult times from which they are learning new preferences. That is natural. But we were never meant to protect people from living the ying and the yang of life experience.

When making decisions, you can't arrive at the answer that feels right for you if you're calibrated to other people. You are only responsible for your own vibration, your own point of attraction. What is *your* truth? Not their truth. If you allow yourself to make the bold assumption that everyone is perfectly cared for by their own inner being and their happiness is not coming from you but from within themselves, you will have more clarity on feeling (tuning) into what you truly desire.

You Can Be Right or You Can Feel Good

Sometimes we have to choose between the two. If your focus is being drawn toward a negative experience and you're reliving it, you may be feeling misunderstood, unappreciated, frustrated, angry, resentful. That is *not* alignment. You have a choice to make: either (A) reach for a better feeling thought or perspective, or (B) make an attempt to get to the bottom of what went wrong. Often, we ruminate about the negative experience, which just attracts more thoughts that are a vibrational match to the frequency of that negative experience. Then your negative momentum is in motion. Or you can stop it early in its tracks and choose to feel good and let go of the need to feel justified in entertaining the negative scenario further. You can't focus on both at the same time, so choosing where you point your focus will determine how you feel and what you are choosing to create as your life, moment by moment.

I had an experience where an Airbnb that I booked was no longer in the pristine condition that it was in when the photos were taken to advertise the property. I reached out to the Airbnb corporate representatives, with photos of mold on the walls, cracked glass in the windows, and dead withered plants that were once green and beautiful. Ultimately, I made peace with the condition of the apartment and decided it was my preference to not change properties at this point in my trip. After Airbnb reviewed the photos I had submitted through their app, I received a 30% refund and I moved on with my vacation. Later, when it came time to write a review of how my experience was, my roommate in the Airbnb was of the strong opinion I should take the photos and publish a scathing review in order to spare future guests the disappointment that we had experienced. But by that point, I was on another law of attraction cruise, happily focusing on new thoughts from the seminar. I decided as I walked down the hall that I could either stop and point my focus back toward the negative experience and be right and justified, or I could choose to stay focused in my present seminar and feel good. It was an easy decision. I was ready to let go of the Airbnb experience because I couldn't focus on both at the same time. Both were true, and both were present in my life. I wanted to deliberately focus on what feels *good*. That's a simple example of asking myself: What kind of momentum do I want to start? How do I want to trend?

See Yourself in a Bigger Way

My second law of attraction cruise was *next level* in every way. By the end of the eight-day cruise, one theme kept presenting itself. I was hearing in different ways that people viewed me very differently than how I viewed myself. I must have needed to learn this because it kept coming up so that I could recognize it as the theme of that seminar cruise experience. It started with a bang. On the first day of the seminar, as it opened up to the audience in its question-and-answer format, most of us raised our hands to be chosen to come up on stage and ask nonphysical wisdom our personal, human question. As Esther scanned the audience for who would kick us off, it was *me*. It felt like I was being launched from a slingshot. It may not seem like a big deal to others, but hundreds of people were hoping to be chosen so it was an honor to have the opportunity. I started the seminar off with my discussion around my decision to treat my next twelve months as a science experiment and have ridiculous amounts of intentional fun. The conversation went on for thirty minutes, which was unusually long.

As the seminar progressed, I received feedback from a friend that when I was up on stage, the people sitting next to her said, "He has such a presence." I thought it was humorous to hear that from other people. Although I do think of myself in a healthy, positive light, my overall perception of myself was on the silly side. I know I'm a good person. I've got a successful career. I'm intelligent. I'm good at what I do. I get lots of comments about my salt and pepper hair . . . lots of good stuff. But mostly I tend to think of myself as a friendly, middle-aged gay guy who is more feminine than I'd like to be. Mostly I don't think about myself. I tend to think about what I'm doing or what I'd like to do next. I definitely think about what I'd like to eat. So, to receive unsolicited feedback like "he has such a presence" pretty much blew my mind and made me laugh.

One morning I was walking around the ship trying to find a quiet place to meditate. I had been all over the boat with no luck. I was on the top deck headed to a seating area when two ladies asked me if I was the guy who spoke about tennis during yesterday's seminar. I walked over to them and said no, that was someone else. I was the first gray-haired guy who talked about having fun. One of the women said, "Oh! I was just telling her I thought you were so advanced and articulate; I could never do that."

Again, I was shocked that *that* was their impression of me. Wow. I had to laugh. It was a little embarrassing but so weird to have such a different image of myself than what others were conveying back to me. I always hate hearing my voice or seeing myself on video. So that's how I saw myself. Clearly none of us are very objective when it comes to judging ourselves. I definitely feel confident in who I am as a human, but I could tell it was important for me to see myself differently in order to manifest a bigger, bolder, more abundant version of the life I desired.

Seeing Myself *Really* Big

Towards the end of the seminar, I learned that KT was an energy coach. It occurred to me to ask her for a private session on board instead of waiting until we were home. I still remember feeling noticeably bolder than usual in asking for what I sensed would be a greatly beneficial experience. The old me would have assumed she considered herself on vacation and therefore it was off limits to ask. I was saying yes to myself by asking for what I wanted. She could always say no.

Before I share my session with KT, I want to explain what makes her so special and why I was so eager to work with her. Simply put, KT has the ability to tune into a person's higher self or inner being (the soul level of your being) and translate the information that is coming directly from that person's eternal, higher self. The result is a back-and-forth conversation with your own nonphysical self. It is the coolest thing ever and I wanted to experience it ASAP!

As KT made her way to our designated meeting location on the top deck of the ship, the session was starting in the sense that my inner being already started coming through. We would normally call this phenomenon channeling, but I haven't met one person who "channels" who agrees with the term "channeling." They all prefer a word like "receiving" to explain what is happening. This makes sense to me now that I've been practicing and studying meditation and the law of attraction in this way. We all are receiving information 24/7, but because it feels so natural, we often mistake the act of receiving this broadcast of never-ending universal intelligence and information as simply "thinking" or maybe as "inspiration." But people like KT are not only aware of this continuous availability of information but are also more practiced in receiving communication in a more profound or deeper way. This is not just the result of each person's "gift"; more importantly, it comes from their expectation that this is possible and available to them. It is available to all of us! Some are simply further down the road of their awareness and therefore tuned in to the information that is flowing to each of us.

So, the information from my inner being was flowing to KT and she then translated *ME* to me. My inner being began by asking me the following:

"How big do you think you are?"

I did not understand the question, so I responded, "I'm awesome."

My IB then responded, "Mmmm, how big do you think you are energetically?"

I didn't even know how to quantify that! This was so outside of any context I was used to so my IB tried again. "How much space would you take up on the boat?"

I answered, "Energetically? I'd fill the whole boat."

My inner being continued. "Now how big do you think you are?"

"I'm spilling out over the rails!"

I could feel my awareness of not knowing how to answer this type of question fade as I relaxed into a flow that was coming from a receiving place instead of my thinking brain.

My inner being went on. "Okay, now, how big do you think you are?"

"Ooooohhhhh . . . As far as the eye can see," I answered. I was starting to get where this was going.

My inner being asked me to say specifically, so I responded, "To the horizon and all around?"

My inner being reminded me that this is about me seeing myself as energy.

"Right. I definitely am picturing energy," I replied.

As this visualizing myself as energy continued, my ability to see myself bigger and bigger continued so that when my inner being asked, "Now how big?" I finally arrived at "I don't really see any boundaries, just all of space."

To which my inner being responded, "Oh my . . . and you got there in thirty seconds."

It only took thirty seconds for me to go from "I have no idea what we are talking about" to "I fill the universe with the energy of my being." My mind was blown.

How fascinating and thrilling to be guided to a new and wider perspective than I would even have known to ask for before this session.

"It's fun to think of new things. Did I do it?" I asked my inner being.

"Of course! You did it. You're guiding the session, not KT. You are guiding the session. It's you, your larger self, 100% running the show."

"Wowww."

My inner being added, "That's who you're talking to right now."

Just when you think it couldn't be more fun, it gets more fun. I was having such an expansive, new sense of momentum before this session and then that happened.

My life was blowing up in such an exciting way—and this turned out to be only the beginning.

Don't Make Other People Wrong.
Don't Make a Situation Wrong.
Don't Make Yourself Wrong.

Just like the food buffet or radio station, we live in a huge, diverse world of people and opinions. Billions of people have lived all kinds of lives and arrived at their own conclusions and preferences. Our vibrational frequency is so much more in alignment with what we really desire when we aren't making other people right or wrong. When we aren't making situations right or wrong. Instead, look at everything as either preferred or not preferred. That is such a lighter way to live your life. Don't beat up on yourself or others when things don't go as perfectly as you'd hoped.

Liz, one of the women that I've worked with as a coach, told a story about missing her flight. As she arrived to discover that her flight was leaving without her, the thought that came to her was "don't make this wrong." I really loved hearing that. What is more productive is to think, "Here I am in this now moment. How do I want to feel? Which feels better? 'I can't believe I missed my fucking flight. This is a nightmare!' or 'Well, of course I never wanted to miss my flight, but I will learn from this. From now on I'll always allow even more time for bad traffic or long security lines.'" Can you imagine how sure-footed, how steady you would feel as you navigate your life if you felt light about everything? If you knew that in the grand scheme of things, everything is not only ok, but great? *This condition or experience in front of me will not be my excuse to not feel good. This situation will not be the reason I am mad at myself. Could it be that even in the presence of this missed flight, I can choose to continue to be aligned with the well-being that is dominant in me and in the universe?* The answer is surprisingly (but beautifully) YES!

Everything Is Always Working Out for Me

"Everything is always working out for me" sounds like a casual, good feeling thought. But really it is a deep, profound law operating in your life on your behalf. Nothing is ever truly going wrong. You are an eternal being who came to this earth to sort and sift through life, experience contrast, and then recognize the preferences born from the life that you are living. Contrast is a word that refers to the buffet of positive and negative feeling experiences or emotions or circumstances. I've heard Abraham speak of contrast as "variety." There is a huge variety of experiences and realities going on around us at all times. We knew when we decided to come into this earthly life that there would be a huge variety of conditions and experiences going on around us. We knew that we would sort and sift through this variety as a way to learn what we preferred. We knew we would create and shape our lives based on what we preferred.

You may be standing in a moment where things are not going your way. We have all been there. When that happens to me now, I have life experience that has shown me that even though it may not appear to be going my way, and even though I can't see it yet, everything is always working out for me. One example of this is when I was buying my dream loft. My final walkthrough before the closing the next day was later than normal. The walkthrough was at 6:00 p.m. When I arrived at the property, I found water dripping from the ceiling in the master bath. I couldn't believe it. What a nightmare. We had to delay the closing so the owners could investigate what was causing it and then fix it. What was uncovered was a malfunctioning part in the HVAC system, which was installed above the ceiling in the master bath. The specific part that was broken or cracked wasn't manufactured as a separate part. This was taking days and burning time. Long story short, the only way to fix it was for the owner to completely replace the HVAC with a brand-new unit. What looked like a situation where everything was going wrong was in fact working out for me. I just couldn't see that in the middle of it. I had no idea that I was going to get a brand-new air conditioning and heating system installed for free. If my closing had been scheduled at the beginning of the day, the mess and confusion of why there was dripping water in my master bath would have been completely my legal responsibility to figure out, install, and pay for. Everything did in fact work out for me. Now I trust that this is always true for me regardless of what I am in the middle of.

Living an Unconditional Life Is True Freedom

If you strive to be unconditional in your joy, to feel good regardless of the circumstances outside of your control, you are living an unconditional life. So even when you are watching your plane take off without you, you can find a better feeling thought by knowing at your core that missing your flight doesn't make you a bad person and it doesn't define your life forevermore. I love this story because we have been raised to automatically have the biggest shit storm reaction to missing a flight. It is so liberating to know I can give myself permission to not beat myself up when something like this happens. The freedom to love myself so much that I can say, "It's ok . . . I'm more than ok in this moment" and mean it. This is what I love most about what I now know. That's what I love about living in this space of loving myself. I have shed all the bullshit I've ever been told or absorbed over my life. So, pardon me while I run around stark raving mad, ridiculously free and unconditionally happy. I love me, I see the big picture, it's blowing my mind, and I'm *never* going back to the old way of looking at life and myself and others. Before I would have been 100% invested in the horror of the inconvenience factor of missing my flight. I would have been 100% tuned into it as a negative condition. A song I hated playing on repeat. Now I'm invested in showing myself unconditional love and patience and softness and kindness. This is true freedom!

We Didn't Come to Fix a Broken World

This concept doesn't require much explanation, but it dramatically impacts how I view the world. We didn't come to this life to fix people or problems because the world isn't broken. Yes, there is drama and tragedy. But we knew before we came into this human experience that there would be a great range and variety of lived experiences on this planet. We didn't require that everything be organized and cleaned up before we arrived. We knew we would move towards the experiences we preferred as we lived life. This is often discussed at the seminars I've attended. As soon as I heard it, I could feel years of worry roll off my shoulders. The earth and universe are ordered by the dominant laws of well-being. The earth has its own momentum, has its own sovereign frequency of well-being. Because this really resonated with me as true, it allowed me to release a sense of burden and feelings of helplessness and doom.

Our Power Is in The Now

We are creating our future in our now. When we make a decision in our now, we are vibrating that point of attraction out into the universe, attracting more of what we are feeling or vibrating. To which the universe responds. For example, if you go to a restaurant and are looking at the menu, what you order is important. If you really want lobster or steak but order something else because it's cheaper, you are telling the universe to send you more compromise, more "doing without." "Universe, please send me my third choice." "Universe, please do not deliver to me what I truly desire." Your decision-making process came from a lens of scarcity, not abundance. You chose by price, not desire or preference. "Universe, send me less than what I really would love." When you choose the meal that you have the most enthusiasm for, you are creating your future in that moment. You are saying, "Universe, send me more of that which I truly desire."

The same is true when we are tuned into how we are feeling. An example of this is when I was in Portofino, Italy, basking in the outrageous beauty of the landscape. I had dreamed of visiting a particular hotel with an iconic view from its outdoor restaurant. I remember thinking, "I want to sit at that table and drink my morning coffee!" Then, after several years of imagining myself there, I had finally said yes and was basking in the beauty of it all. I realized that right then and there, seated at that table and basking in appreciation of the experience, I was telling the universe, "I want to feel more of this feeling." I was creating my future at that moment. I was broadcasting a signal of appreciation that was being responded to by the universe. The law of attraction responds to our now feeling. That is how our "now" creates our future life. When we are mostly consistent in the higher frequency emotions of appreciation, love, and joy (the emotion of fun), we are trending powerfully. Then our trending isn't the old split energy of reacting to life in a knee-jerk response kind of way, which slows down our ability to attract what we desire. When we practice choosing how we want to feel regardless of the conditions happening around us, we broadcast more consistently (are a vibrational match to) the higher frequencies of abundance and well-being.

Game Changer

Our potential for leveraging our greatest power is by understanding that our inner being is focused with us at all times and on the same subject that we are focused upon. Even the most insignificant experience or detail. When we are holding the same opinion or perspective that our inner being holds on whatever we are focused on, we feel good, we feel positive emotion. When we diverge from the opinion our inner being holds on any subject, person, or situation, we feel negative emotion. As an example, let's say you go to the grocery store to purchase Diet Coke, and none are in stock. If you feel frustrated or angry (negative emotion), that is evidence that your inner being is focused right there with you, is aware of the same details but does not share your perspective of frustration because our inner being isn't dependent on outside conditions to feel good. I love knowing that my inner being is involved in 100% of everything I'm experiencing. No matter how trivial. So, when we are aligned with our inner being, we feel good. Feeling happy and satisfied means we have the energy of the universe flowing through us. We are tuned to the power that creates worlds. Those who are not in alignment with Source Energy are using human effort to accomplish what they desire. In one of the seminars I attended, Abraham compared human "efforting" to an attempt to vacuum your carpet without plugging in the vacuum cleaner to the electric current. You're going through the motions of cleaning your carpet but are not leveraging the power available to you and, therefore, you are accomplishing nothing. But for those who are plugged into their Source Energy, they are more powerful than millions who are not.[1]

My Knowing

Of all the beautiful things I've manifested or created, my favorite possession is the knowing of the concepts in this section. The thrill I feel simply walking down the street knowing that I'm way more than a physical body with a list of errands to accomplish. Knowing how I relate to this magical universe is something I wouldn't trade for all the money in the world.

Note

1.   Abraham Hicks, Abraham Hicks Alaska cruise seminar, Aug. 2021.

Chapter 4

UNICORN SHIT

I THINK IT'S HELPFUL TO SHARE MY OWN EXAMPLES OF THE negative energy I experienced at the beginning of my journey and how I turned it around. I was then applying what I was learning to everyday situations in real time. Abraham says often that "words don't teach, life experience teaches." Once you connect the dots for yourself with the specifics and details of your own life, you have integrated the concepts, and it becomes your truth. Then you are living from a place of knowing versus seeking.

Please Tell Me That My Inner Being Is Pissed at This Shit

I had discussed this with my partner. We had agreed. Yet there I was looking at splatters all over the toilet bowl. I could feel the blood boiling anger that was starting to build. *I guess I just need to have NO standards and life would be easier.* As I started to escalate *not* in the direction of abundance and joy, the thought presented itself to me: "My inner being isn't feeling angry about this and his inner being doesn't care either." This stopped me in my tracks. *Let me take that in*, I thought. Well fuck, that changed everything. I could feel how radical a shift this new perspective was. I had been banging my head against this particular wall of "men are oblivious assholes." I assure you it was most definitely working against me. Not because it wasn't "true." But because it had been splitting my energy! This was a constant, recurring wall of frustration. When I would arrive at this angry feeling place, I would always feel lost. It never felt like the right answer to just lower my standards to no standards at all. Sure, if I expected inconsiderate cohabiting, then I could be happy as a pig in slop. That never felt like a satisfying solution. In my mind, I had already lowered my standards beyond anything I felt was reasonable. But this new perspective was life changing. Since my inner being and his inner being saw him as a magnificent being, this toilet event was a non-event. Holy shit . . . literally and figuratively.

Annoyed as Fuck Is a Frequency

The act of choosing better-feeling thoughts still required practice and repetition. An ongoing "condition" of frustration for me was our large entry hall. It was long and wide and had the potential to be an important and beautiful part of what we loved about our loft. Every room in a loft is important since there are (by definition) not many rooms in a loft. It had been *months* and little boxes of junk were parked in our entry hall and completely off his radar. Guess whose radar they were on every time I sat in my home office at the other end of the long hallway? Yep. ME. Every time I went in or out, I was aware of how junky it looked compared to how good it could feel. And the beautiful part of this to me was it's not that I was wrong!! It was objectively dumb to live with this crap when it could easily be attended to. But being right is different than feeling good.

One of my favorite concepts in this whole law of attraction thing is "in every particle of the universe, there is wanted and unwanted."

You can look at something unwanted or negative and it can be true and real. But there is also "wanted" right there in the same particle. Your choice is to decide which you are going to focus on. You can't focus on both at the same time. And your focus on "unwanted" will attract more unwanted, whereas your focus on "wanted" will attract more wanted. Whatever subject you think about, you join or tune to that vibration. You activate that vibration. Annoyed as fuck at hall clutter is most definitely a vibration. That vibration was now my point of attraction. See how this works? However, in that moment, I wasn't thinking *any* of this. What I was thinking was, "He's had long enough to deal with this shit, and not only have I had it, but I'm also going to move it all out into the common area hall just beyond our front door and he can deal with it there when he's *finally* fuckin' ready."

Right on the heels of that thought came an audio clip from a video I'd watched earlier. It played in my head: "Be lighthearted and playful about your life." Well fuck me. I thought, "That's not *at all* what I'm doing right now. I'm not feeling lighthearted about my life." The good news is I hadn't consciously "asked" but I definitely received my answer from my inner being. And I was ready to hear it. Even though I was headed down a negative spiral, my answer came as a result of the good momentum I had been predominantly living.

So, I chose to focus in on the positive or "wanted" that was present in that hallway. Although I didn't see a silver lining from the clutter still parked there, I could find a way to let it go. As mentioned earlier, a helpful concept I've learned is that you can choose to be right or to feel good. This is so often the case in life. I could see the wisdom in choosing to feel good versus being right in this example. In this moment, and with great intention or focus, I was finding a way to "be lighthearted." I was looking for and finding an opportunity to choose "playful." Tuning deliberately to an attitude of "everything is ok and eventually this will all get sorted" is a way different vibration than feeling exasperated and resentful. This was doing the work of attracting abundance, well-being, and joy into my life. I knew that this was a revolutionary shift in how I was deliberately choosing to look at my life.

Choices at The Four Seasons

One morning while on vacation, I sipped my latte on a beautiful cafe patio at the Four Seasons. Tranquil mornings outside with a cup of coffee in hand are my favorite part of any day. As I sat appreciating the cool morning and basking in a truly perfect moment, a woman sitting at the table next to me finished eating and started to call one girl-friend after another to catch up and shoot the breeze. Nothing impor-tant, just idle chat to stave off boredom, I guessed. I thought everyone understood talking on your cell phone at a restaurant was rude and inconsiderate. They even have signs on the Chicago subway asking pas-sengers to refrain from cell phone conversations. As my blood started to boil, I remembered this was a choice. I couldn't control what others did in the world, but I could control how I felt. I can choose how I feel. This was the perfect opportunity to apply a quote from *Getting into the Vortex*, an Abraham Hicks meditation: "Since you can't change others to please you, appreciating them where they are will give you ease." I could feel myself relax. It felt so good to have a new tool to use. This really was helpful information to have at my disposal and the feeling of accomplishment within me was exhilarating. I was doing it! I was being a deliberate creator by choosing to think better-feeling thoughts. If that woman knew she was being tacky and rude, she wouldn't do what she was doing. Or maybe she would. The important thing was I could appreciate her where she was and that did give me ease.

Had I allowed myself to continue to be annoyed in that moment, I would not have been tuned to the frequency of appreciation and abundance. I would have been focused on problems, not solutions. Bliss brings abundance and fault-finding finds more faults. Now I was feeling true freedom. When others around you can ruin your experience, you are a victim. Victims are rarely wealthy, and they certainly aren't happy. And I want to be happy.

In every moment we are either moving toward what we desire, or we are moving away from it. And what we vibrate attracts the vibrational match to that vibration. Bliss attracts bliss and the things and thoughts and experiences that match a blissful state. Have you ever noticed when you feel angry and frustrated, everyone in traffic is so annoying? Or things keep going wrong all around you and you can't seem to catch a break? That's momentum. That's why I'm choosing the thought that feels best in each moment. "She doesn't know she's being tacky and rude, or she wouldn't do it" felt better than "I hate that dumb bitch . . . she's ruining my peaceful morning and it is literally her fault." And "I can't control other people's behavior and appreciating them where they are gives me ease" felt way better too.

This wasn't a one-and-done. I'm still applying this almost every day in my relationship. But being aware of *why* it's important, and *how*, impacts not only how good I'm feeling but also if I'm moving in the direction and energy of abundance. Being deliberate about what I think and how I choose to view events in my life is truly being a deliberate creator versus reacting to life randomly. I was realizing that thinking some situations in life feel good and some feel really bad was a conditional way of living and responding. I can't control the conditions around me, but I can control how I feel about my life moment by moment. That's taking ownership of how I feel. That's true freedom. Other people don't have to behave the way I want them to in order for me to feel good. Part of my feeling unshakeable and sure-footed as I navigate life is knowing that there is actually no such thing as good or bad. There just is. And I can instead look at whatever is happening in front of me as either preferred or unpreferred. That removes a world of judgment. Nothing has to be wrong anymore, it can exist as simply not my preference. I can let go of trying to manage how or what other people are doing and just be responsible for what I'm doing and feeling. These are not new ideas. These concepts have been taught in Buddhist teachings and countless other philosophies. Clearly most aren't living this way, but I've heard similar concepts being discussed recently by yoga teachers, for example. How do I *want* to move through the world? How do I want to feel, react, respond, attract?

My Own Missed Flight— The Practice of Not Making It Wrong

While retelling one of my travel adventures, I realized that I had had my own missed flight story where I showed myself I could be unconditional. I had flown from Sydney to my connecting airport in the South Pacific island of Port Vila. My friend Zonda had invited me to her beautiful resort on the neighboring island of Santo. When I had organized my flights, she advised me to avoid staying overnight in Port Vila. This was in the back of my mind as the customer service agent told me I had missed my flight from Port Vila to Santo because I was late and therefore my flight was canceled and rescheduled for the next day. I showed the woman my travel itinerary and that I was checking in an hour ahead of schedule.

Then she changed her story and said it was rescheduled due to weather conditions. I was confused. I was so eager to get to my final destination and couldn't believe what was happening. I had chartered a tiny puddle jumper to complete this final leg of my journey. I was the only client, so this didn't make sense. There was nothing left for me to try and I surrendered to the turn of events. Then the customer service woman told me they had booked me into a hotel and would put me on a bus. I insisted that I would take a taxi. This was a third world country, and I wasn't in the mood to navigate a scorchingly hot form of public transportation.

"There aren't any taxis."

I was incredulous. "This is an airport . . . there have to be taxis!"

Nope. No taxis. I was definitely not in Milan or Paris. (Which actually ended up making this whole trip so special. The contrast and ruggedness of it all. But that appreciation came later.)

She led me to a van where a nice man was ready to take me to my hotel. As I drove in this van to my hotel, I decided that everything was ok. I wasn't going to let this change in plans make me feel upside down. I knew feeling secure in my joy was always available and true regardless of the circumstances I found myself plopped into. After I checked in and got to my room, I spotted a small critter on my bedside table. OMG was that a tiny scorpion? Whew, no. It was some sort of lizard. I attempted to shoo it away but instead it ran the opposite direction towards the pillows on my bed. Still, I maintained that everything was A-OK, and I would just appreciate all of it as my exotic adventure on my way to Zonda's beautiful beach resort.

I love that I had this experience to show myself I could navigate a missed flight of my own and tune in to the radio station playing "It's ok, I'm ok, nothing has gone wrong." I was much happier in that frequency than the frequency of "freak out and outrage." Both frequencies were available to tune to, so I'm glad I had already been trending toward feeling sure-footed and joyous.

Chapter 5

UNICORN MILESTONES

THIS CHAPTER IS A COLLECTION OF BREAKTHROUGH MOMENTS. And although they don't flow from one to another in the way a continuous story would, they serve as an important way for me to share my unicorn journey and the important moments when I expanded and became more. One beautiful new awareness at a time. These are the manifestations that were the result of applying my experiment of fun to the details of my life. A manifestation can range from feeling an emotional response to a new awareness to a physical thing you've been desiring showing up in your life.

The Big Tip

As I look back to a day in the magnificent park in St. Louis, I realize it was a tipping point. As I walked in the sunshine around a grand reflecting pool, I listened to the songs that always sent me soaring. I could feel a bigger, more expansive feeling of alignment. It was unlike anything I had felt before. My coach, KT, texted me to tell me she could sense that I was in a high-flying place by how big my energy was at that moment. She was in Oregon, and I was in Missouri, but that was KT's special gift. Once she had translated my nonphysical self in a session, she would continue to feel connected to my energy. That was the case for all her clients.

When I got home, my partner had his own breakthrough to report. But first a little background. At the beginning of the pandemic, he had lost his job. We were forced to wait it out regarding looking for a new job. He had decided that he would start freelancing again when COVID was no longer an issue. I agreed that he should ride out the worst part of the pandemic before trying to work again. Becoming a freelance stylist again would allow him to create his own schedule with the flexibility that would allow him to travel whenever we wanted.

During the Pacific Coast cruise (our second cruise), my partner had met several potential clients. Once they met him and learned he had a background in fashion as a stylist and personal shopper, they wanted to work with him.

When we were home, one of our friends from the cruise called on the phone to catch up with my partner and asked him if he wanted to join her on her trip to New York City. She offered to pay him his hourly rate and pay for his airfare and hotel expenses. Holy Fuckballs! I had spent more than a year working diligently on myself to see my partner as not stuck and lacking motivation. I had learned from my study of the law of attraction that we needed to calibrate not to where we were at but to where we wanted to go. I needed to write a new story and hold that in my thought as my reality even if it hadn't manifested yet in physical form. I knew my partner was talented, and his nonphysical self was not blocked or shut off from abundance but was truly thriving! This had gone on for about a year and a half and now look at *this*! He manifested a client who was willing to not only pay him his sizable hourly rate but also pay for his airfare and hotel too. Our future state vision of what success looked like for him had officially manifested. This truly was his dream job scenario and so soon! I was just as happy for me as I was for him. This was my victory too.

I remember playing an Abraham-Hicks game, or what they call a "process," right before we left for that second cruise. It's called "Wouldn't it be fun if . . ." It allows you to be specific about dreaming big but in a playful way. I had specifically written, "Wouldn't it be fun if my partner met someone on the cruise who was looking for someone with his exact work experience? Wouldn't it be fun if he met his next employer?" Over the last one and a half years of his under employment, I had not given up hope. I had stayed focused on where we were going, not where we were. Now both of us had experienced our individual and collective tipping points.

My months of studying ideas in a book, ideas in my head, had now exploded onto the scene where I could actually see it and experience it with my physical senses. I could see all the details of my deliberate creation move from thought into the physical details of my life. WOW! I was now feeling my own success viscerally as fact. And it wasn't about money (although I love money). It was about feeling invincible and unstoppable and the power of clarity. As mentioned earlier, Abraham often says that "words don't teach, life experience teaches."

Bring It into the Now

After that Pacific Coast cruise, I started texting one of the new friends I had met. On the ship, she was describing to a group of us in the coffee bar how she had several ideas for t-shirts that would use language normally associated with addiction and recovery but would be applied in a new way. On the spot I felt led to say I would design them for her. She accepted my offer, and we agreed it would be fun to get to know each other and brainstorm other ideas together in a location that was somewhere between our two home cities.

So, once I got back home and we were chatting via text, we said, "Wouldn't it be fun to run away together?" Seriously, let's do it! Let's do exactly that! We can return to our partners after four days with our tails not so tucked between our legs. Outside of the nearly out of body clarity and mandate to act that I had felt about booking the Alaska cruise, this was the purest feeling of YES energy I had felt in moving forward with new plans. It was so easy to say yes. So, I looked at flights for various cities to see what was convenient (and *warm*!). We agreed on Phoenix, Arizona. And when we arrived, that YES energy was still active and fully in force.

Abby and I complemented each other perfectly. We each had such certainty and were so practiced in our own fields of expertise that we moved effortlessly through decisions about what we wanted to focus on first and then moved effortlessly through the specifics of those project details. We had every intention of working with such ease and a feeling of little to no effort. It was astonishing to witness it unfold in real time. We were so pleased and delighted that our idea of merging work and play was as wonderful as we'd hoped. We were in our unicorn magic!

At one point it really hit me as I looked at our laptops open and back-to-back on a table under a tree near the pool bar. What I had dreamed of hadn't taken five years to realize. I was living it already. It felt like it snuck up on me. I knew I was continuing my quest for non-stop travel and fun by planning this long weekend in sunny Phoenix, but seeing our laptops set up under the shade of this beautiful tree at the pool really blew my mind. I was actually working and on vacation at the same time. I had pulled my big dreams of the future into my now. It's hard to describe how it feels when the dream becomes reality, but the expression of pinching yourself to see if you're dreaming comes really close.

Each morning after breakfast and before I'd settle into working at my laptop, I'd take ten to fifteen minutes to walk along the beautiful trails while I listened to my favorite songs. I still can't get over how exalted I felt while listening to the lyrics and music as I would take in the exotic desert landscape. It was thrilling to process that I was far from home on vacation again and so soon. I was soaring in appreciation for the magic I was living. How astonishing that felt. I'm 100% addicted to this feeling of exhilaration. I appreciate knowing this is what I feel when I am aligned with the fullness of my being.

To feel the beautiful temperature and hear the lyrics of pure swagger reinforcing my soaring spirit was better than anything my future millions would one day buy. But I'm excited to have both. And I'm clear that this is the clarity and powerful emotion that will make that abundance possible. This feeling is the magnet that attracts all that I desire right to me.

It was intoxicating to be so confident and feel such clarity around the success we were there to create together. During our first day we moved so quickly through our decisions it was laughable. After dinner, we ended our day reading tarot cards by the hotel fireplace. I sipped on a chocolate martini (it was tradition now). The cards reinforced the success of our endeavors. We decided to focus the next morning on redesigning Abby's logo and coming up with new colors for her.

Lucky Fucker

The next morning, I was enjoying how comfortable my bed was and not quite ready to get up. Suddenly I saw a visual of Abby's new logo in my mind. Holy shit! My eyes widened in amazement, and I happily sprang out of bed to make a quick sketch to capture what I saw. Now that is an exhilarating way to start any day. Wow, I was sure that had never happened to me before. I had always heard stories of songwriters having their song or lyrics come to them word for word in a matter of minutes and go on to sell millions of records. I always thought they were lucky fuckers, and it wasn't fair. But there I was . . . ME . . . a lucky fucker!

The momentum continued. It was effortless and thrilling. I showed my sketch to Abby, and she squealed in approval. We had another sit-down breakfast and then went outside to set up our computers again in the shade by the pool bar. On the heels of having Abby's logo magically shown to me in a vision, I took my walk strutting to my songs even more buoyant than before. I felt like I just couldn't make a mistake.

Walk This Way

Later in the afternoon, Abby left to get a hot tea. As she left the pool area, the gate closed and locked behind her. She realized she had forgotten to bring her phone or key card. Although she wasn't overly worried about it, she was wondering how she was going to get back in. She proceeded to order her tea and as she returned, what did she see? Ahead of her was the door to the pool standing wide open. What's amusing is that the gate was engineered with a spring and magnet to automatically close.

She didn't have to ask someone from the hotel to let her in or look for another guest to open the gate. She didn't have to try and flag me down to come to her aid. All she had to do was move forward and walk in the direction she wanted to go. Everything was already taken care of. This may seem like a small event, but it is exactly the same for the big events we care so much about. This was a powerful example of how our path could luxuriously unfold if we only knew to expect to live in unicorn magic. We are that loved and that worthy, and the universe is not only ready but wants to yield to us every detail both large and small.

I so appreciate what I've learned, what I know. I appreciate the clarity and joy of alignment. I love knowing life is supposed to be fun. I love knowing I get to feel good all the time and to choose deliberately the thoughts I think. I am not just regurgitating what's going on around me. I am not unintentionally recreating the same reality over and over. I am the deliberate creator of my experience. I am choosing to create something new by looking for and reaching beyond what currently exists. How I feel and what I think about each subject in my life is up to me. I am not in control of how people behave or what's going on around me, but I get to control how I feel and think about it. Since my first and most important relationship is with myself, I look to myself for joy, satisfaction, appreciation, respect, worthiness, and love. If I'm good with me, it doesn't matter if others are good with me. I don't need validation from outside conditions or other people. I am working on me, and what others do and feel is none of my business.

The more I've understood this, the less I'm pulled into someone else's bad mood or attitude. I'm steady regardless of someone else's unsteadiness. One of the early concepts that helped me find my steadiness was the idea that I can't change others to please me. Full stop. Repeat, I can't change others to please me. Accepting others where they are on their journey gives me a feeling of ease, peace, and acceptance.

From the Great Beyond: My Mom

On the trip, Abby had shared her experience using a spirit guide meditation that resulted in such vivid encounters with her spirit guides that I was quite envious. So, I listened to a guided meditation on our trip before breakfast one morning. I didn't have the tangible results she experienced but I chalked it up to my beginner status and stayed light and open as I eased into this new world. Each morning I would decide which meditation I would listen to. Most mornings it was my favorite Abraham-Hicks meditation but occasionally I would reach for the spirit guide meditation by Gabby Bernstein.

Since it was Thanksgiving morning and I had the day off, I decided to try the spirit guide meditation again. I felt easy about it and understood that my desire to connect with my mom would come gradually. I had already agreed with myself to not add pressure by expecting to make immediate contact. Previously when the meditation said, "Ask your spirit guides their names," and no names came through, I didn't sweat it. There was plenty to enjoy with the music included in the guided meditation in addition to simply enjoying how it felt to meditate. Besides, I had such an exciting morning already. I had woken with a direct phrase placed inside my head for my book. It was unmistakable even for someone like me who doesn't normally receive "messages" or "downloads" from what I would call spiritual consciousness. I had jumped up and written for close to two hours. After experiencing all of that excitement, I was especially inspired to sit down and meditate.

As I closed my eyes and turned inward, I felt so happy and appreciative of what had already happened. It is always thrilling to feel direct guidance from Spirit. As I eased into the guided meditation, I could feel a soft but sudden shift from thinking into feeling. I wasn't repeating wonderful concepts or mantras but instead I was just feeling purely tapped into a state of Love. Love which is surely divine. I felt so good. Because it was a guided meditation, there were a series of prompts throughout. One was to ask your spirit guides to reveal their names and then a prompt to thank them for providing their wisdom and guidance. The meditation then reached the last section where you could sit for several minutes soaking up the beautiful, ethereal music and the bliss that had been building.

And then it happened. I felt the smallest possible awareness that had not been there before. An awareness that wasn't general but specific to a knowing that my mother was present. Tears welled up in my eyes and I started sobbing quietly. I felt such a feeling of relief and enormous joy. I felt so many things all at once. Years of intellectually understanding that she was always with me gave way to this beautiful sensing of our first contact.

It had been twenty-two years since she had died suddenly. I had longed for this spiritual reunion. I was overwhelmed. Now it was happening because I was feeling higher in vibration than ever. Feeling—not thinking. I felt the significance of that mental shift and the dots being connected. It felt wonderful to understand the causation behind what I was experiencing. My patience had paid off and now I could see the progress I was making. I was in what is called the receiving mode. I was in the state of allowing and that's why a piece of my book woke me which then continued to the most beautiful reunion with my amazing mother.

The guided meditation included writing the thoughts that came in the few minutes following the meditation. Here's what I wrote:

"Thank you, spirit guides. Mama, I'm relaxing into feeling your divine Love essence and presence. I will commune with you here and listen. I love you so much. I know you were always with me, and I trust my path. I trust the universe calling me as I'm ready. Life is so beautiful. This is a day to truly give thanks. Even though every day is this beautifully blessed, I love knowing our communication is growing clearer each day. I know we were never separated."

Tears welled up and waves of joy washed over me. Words failed me.

I texted KT to tell her what happened. Just typing the text brought me to tears again. I sat in appreciation for a few more moments and reached for my music. I was drawn to a song called "Amazing" by One EskimO. It captured this new feeling of exaltation perfectly. Little did I know that this song would return to play an important role in the months to come.

I loved these mornings that started off with a bang. I realized that our inner beings can flow mind-blowing wonderful things to us continuously since the universe is infinite. This stream of surprise and delight isn't supposed to end. I accepted and expected this to be my new normal.

Assignment: Mom Meditation

A few months later, I was in a session with my inner being (as translated through KT) and we were discussing my mom. As we were wrapping up the session, I received a homework suggestion.

"When you're in meditation, ask your mom how it feels to be Source Energy, pure Source Energy with no physical body. That will be a very fun ride, a very enjoyable journey for you."

Wow. This was exciting. I tried to do the homework meditation that evening but nothing flowed into my consciousness, so I tried again first thing the next morning (my normal meditation time). My meditation practice was to do an intense, advanced breathwork exercise from Wim Hoff on YouTube. That always left me feeling peaceful and relaxed. As I sat in silence following the breathwork, I could feel that deep energy in my head as I reached out to ask, "Mom, what does it feel like to be Source Energy with no physical body?" My eyes were closed, and waves of energy were swirling in my head. Nothing specific came.

I continued focusing on the sound of the furnace air, happy and expectant. It kept occurring to me to reach for my phone and listen to "Let It Be" by the Beatles but I resisted. I thought, "I don't need a song as a crutch, I know I can always hear Source without other factors being necessary." New distracting thought-chatter would enter, and I would regain my focus. Finally, I picked up my phone to listen to the Beatles song that I had been beautifully guided to several months earlier. I hadn't listened to this song since my session the night before where we discussed my mom in more detail. Whenever my nonphysical self says I'm going to have a cool and special experience, I know it will be true. I was eager. As I listened, that deep, soul resonance transported me immediately. Now, I rarely cry. Not because I'm trying to avoid feeling anything unpleasant. It's just how I'm wired. I would never squelch feeling all the feelings of a movie or situation because I was embarrassed. I don't believe in holding back and missing out on the fullness of an experience. But this song and its use of my mother's name gets to me profoundly. I get so choked up when I hear Paul McCartney sing about Mother Mary. Those lyrics were inspired from Source Energy, received by Paul, and continue to retain that beautiful energy.

As I heard the ending lyrics, I doubled over in emotion, silently sobbing. I wasn't crying from grief or loss but the beauty and sacredness of my love for my mother, for the soul connection that is still powerfully in place. It's a unique emotion that I'm still trying to articulate. It's not exaggerated bliss or peace. It's something else. Whatever it is, I love feeling it. As that song ended, I understood that I had been directed to it as a priming of my emotional pump for what was next in this special meditation homework journey. Immediately I was led to listen to "Amazing" by One EskimO. This song had occurred to me earlier, but I had resisted it as well. It's funny. Somehow, I had an idea in my head of how this was supposed to go down without even realizing it. I just assumed I was supposed to ask and then receive a message of words that answered or showed me the answer. Maybe a trippy, cosmic vision with words or "knowing."

Listening to songs that were already in my iPod playlist felt like a crutch or as though I was missing the message altogether. But I will give myself credit for staying "light" and "guidable." I hit play on this next song. I couldn't believe my ears. Holy Shit this was not a drill. This was sacred ground! Even though I had enjoyed this song as one of my favorites for launching me into my vortex, suddenly it was brand fucking new. Remember, this song was the answer to the question: "Mom, how does it feel to be Source Energy with no physical body?"

I kid you not. The lyrics state that she has no skin but feels everything. HOLY SHIT. I love it when life surprises me. This was not at all what I was expecting. After listening, I understood so many wonderful things from this. One huge understanding was that moving forward, I would not be alone but would feel a new sense of not only my mother, but also my father and grandmother and other nonphysical beings present with me, moving with me everywhere I went. In my coaching sessions, I had just started to go deeper into this understanding that we all are surrounded by nonphysical beings 24/7, lovingly focused on us every moment. I had always known intellectually that my mother was with me but now I could feel it more viscerally. Softly but powerfully.

The Magic Continues

As this experience soaked in, I was led to go to YouTube and type these words in the search bar "flying in space meditation music." Again, don't ask me why those words came, but I was in what is called "receptive mode" where information, knowing, guidance, ideas, and so on flow into the mind. Of the search results, I was drawn to the first two videos. The title of the first video, which was a guided meditation, was especially calling me: "Meditation: Trusting Your Intuition." I mean, c'mon! The second video in the search results was tempting me because it was closer to my initial desire to fly through space with my mom. But the wording "trusting your intuition" was the chef's kiss and I proceeded to follow that magical "Amazing" song with this next video along my trail of divine breadcrumbs.[1]

As I started to listen, I understood that I was going on this guided meditation *with* my mother. It made logical sense that each part of my morning "mom meditation" was building on each other. I was already in my vortex and completely aligned as I listened to each instructional step flowing to me, guiding me.

Within the guided meditation video, I was to ask my intuition a question. What did I want to ask and receive?" I asked my spirit posse to "turn on within me the ability to see and feel with clarity my path to everything I desire: ease, abundance, freedom, fun, alignment. Allow me to see and feel, in exaggerated clarity, my path forward ablaze with light. And the ability to joyously, fearlessly skip along my beautiful trail of choices in confidence, strength, and clarity." I received an image of a red sporty convertible holding me and my spirit world entourage, flying down a hill joyously, our arms up in the air like we were riding a roller coaster at an amusement park.

Releasing Negative Childhood Memories

Next, I was prompted to project any negative childhood memories to the screen. An image surfaced of me sitting on the floor of my bedroom with my sister's Barbie doll. The doll was naked. I was using a long strip of bright red fabric to wrap around her and somehow make it look like she was wearing a beautiful dress. I didn't have the words for it then but basically, I was attempting what we could call a red-carpet worthy dress. My mom entered the room and asked me gently why I liked playing with the Barbie doll. Immediately I realized I was doing something she didn't like or that she felt was wrong. Perhaps my dad was in on this too. I imagine they must have talked about it. This was projected onto the screen.

Next came a memory of me in the college dining room carrying my tray of food over to my table. Suddenly I heard mocking, kissing sounds directed at me. It was coming from a table full of jocks. I had been mostly oblivious that I came across as "different" or feminine. It felt like my happy bubble had been burst wide open in front of everyone. I was humiliated. Decades of society's jeers were projected on screen. Those hurtful memories reduced and transferred off the screen and back into my body, where they were gathered and then released into oblivion.

This meditation process had me observe, then minimize, then release from my body all these different negative thoughts or perspectives I still unknowingly carried and held within me. Even if I was 95% on board with loving myself, the fact that I could even identify these negative perspectives about myself was evidence that they still existed and needed to go. I had realized that unconditional love included my loving myself just as I would love anyone else regardless of their body shape and condition. I realized that I needed to celebrate every single thing about me as perfect and not needing to change. I had no problem with other men being feminine or other women being masculine, so it was way past time that I afford myself the same unconditional acceptance. And not just acceptance, but absolute appreciation!

Like Jack Black

I recall seeing an image of Jack Black in a Mexican wrestling outfit where he was not trying to hide his chubby physique. In fact, it was kind of the point. He was truly glorious in presenting himself that way. I loved that there was no sense of "I'm wearing clothes that flatter me and make me look closer to men that are more fit and desirable." He was shirtless and projecting badass, superhero vibes. Nowhere was there evidence that he thought he was anything less than perfection. *That* was how I wanted to feel moving forward. I could feel the negative energy shrink inside me. This felt like a shift in how I perceived myself. Picturing myself as moving through the world with golden, shimmering light inside me felt new and like the world had to respond to me differently than it did before.

When I had that expansive view of myself on the cruise ship with KT as radiating energy that filled the universe, it was truly a game changer. Now I was going inward, and my human vessel was filled up from within.

Interestingly, I had felt like I had had a blood transfusion the Sunday before when two of my closest friends announced they were now a couple. I had the specific sensation that felt like every cell of my body was glowing in this energy of HUGE, universal Divine Love. I felt illuminated by sparkling light and love. This experience added to, and shored up, that earlier sensation and perception of myself as a powerful attractor moving through the world.

Move to the Better

The next day following this amazing meditation experience, I couldn't wait to discuss it with my inner being.

As the session began there was some fine tuning with my AirPods and iPhone so that KT, translating already as my inner being, could hear more clearly. I changed from my speaker phone to my AirPods and they confirmed that they could hear me more clearly.

Then they made a profound point. Sometimes in life we have a situation that is ok, perfectly fine. But often we have the ability to reach for something far, far better. They used the difference in the audio quality to make this point about the situations we face on a daily basis.

The first way they could hear me. And it was okay. They could understand me. But by requesting an improvement, they achieved a far better audio experience. They wanted me to remember that it's those simple choices in life that would dramatically impact my experience. "Well, this way is good. But often there's far better available. So, I'm going to give myself permission to jump to the far better."

They then used the example of pretending you are stopped at a traffic light in a car you like. When you see a car pull up next to you that you like even better, get out of your current car (even when you have not reached your destination) and allow yourself to move to the new car that is an improvement. I always have the freedom to get out of one car and get into another that I like even better. I should always, always, always trust myself and go to the better feeling. Go to the better thought, go to the better anything. Go to the better! I give myself that permission.

This discussion on choosing the better was only the beginning of a wild, mind-blowing meditation experience. I had been considering the songs I kept feeling encouraged to listen to and the power they had upon me. This led me to ask my inner being about how it all unfolded. It's not what I expected at all. It was so surprising because I'd already heard those songs. It was exciting to know that I could be in the flow. I could listen for and receive each step and then do it even though it felt completely illogical.

Amazing

And so, my question to my inner being was this: Did my mom, who is nonphysical, specifically inspire the songwriter of "Amazing" to receive that specific message so they could relay it to me now?

The answer came back: "Yes."

It was fun, because that was part of the knowing or "download" I had received. And I knew that. This was the first experience I could remember where instead of hearing an answer in words, that piece of it came as just something that was simply known to me, as if my awareness software had been updated and there was now new information in me that wasn't there before.

My inner being asked me why I asked if I already knew that was true. Since this had never happened to me before, I wanted the fun of having nonphysical confirm it for me.

This meditation experience was a perfect example of intentional, deliberate creation. *I'm going to specifically do something and anything can come into my physical experience with a new perspective, a new awareness, or a new message for me. I'm going to go on this voyage with my mom for example.* And then I intentionally focused on seeing and hearing the song through my mom's perspective. And I realized it was her giving me the message. My inner being told me, "It's in as receptive a mode as a human being could have been."

Wow. I felt so honored, excited, and proud of myself to know that!

My mom was literally speaking directly to me, but instead of a human voice it was all imparted vibrationally. Feeling her vibrations, feeling everything, feeling me feeling the feelings in my body, feeling the music, feeling the vibe of the music.

It was exhilarating to be told by my inner being that I was in the perfect receptive mode and that I had achieved what so many humans think is an illusion. I felt so proud and appreciative that I was getting this feedback. I thought I simply had had a once-in-a-lifetime mystical experience. But I was being shown what had happened energetically "behind the scenes." They explained that I often get into receptive mode and that I'm in the vortex every day. In and out, in and out, in and out. But because I had received this homework assignment to deliberately go into meditation to ask my mom how it felt to be non-physical, by doing this, I was going into receptive mode with deliberate intent. I was going into my vortex where I was "wide open to intentional, extraordinary creation." They explained that this is the magnitude, the best of the best, the best of what I came for, the best of what I'm great at . . . playing at. My inner being asked me, "Do you realize and give yourself credit that you're getting better and better and better at playing vibrationally?"

My inner being wanted to make a really clear point. They told me that that a-ha realization that I had when they told me I was in perfect receptive mode was all I needed every day. That one a-ha, that one extraordinary moment in meditation or moment in life or moment of awareness of where I feel source flowing through me so fully and freely. And where all of a sudden, a bird that I've seen a thousand times is the most beautiful creature I've ever seen. That is seeing through my nonphysical eyes. There's no need to constantly chase . . . anything. There's no need to chase anything or wonder if I have done enough or if I'm meditating enough or if I'm chasing this or that enough.

It's that one moment that does more vibrationally than anything else I could be doing. That does more vibrationally for me and my eternal journey than going and sitting in an ashram and not speaking for an entire weekend.

So, the session ended with that . . . the richness of it. The awareness that I intentionally called my mom and that I was just going to keep having an a-ha after a-ha after A-HA. I'm that clear and that powerful of a deliberate creator. I'm that much in receptive mode. I literally just called my mom, who's dead by the way. But she came through so clearly. I went on this journey with her because that was the desire of my heart.

My inner being ended the session with, "You have that kind of ability. Yeah, you do. That state of being. It's that feeling you're always after."

This was an experience I will never forget.

You Are Loved

One morning, as I opened my eyes, the words came to me, "You are loved."

Interesting! I knew I was loved but to hear it directly from Source Energy felt new and life changing. I say life changing because then there was so much more color and depth to this feeling of being loved. On the heels of receiving "you are loved" was an understanding that went with it that I was going to receive something. Like it was the announcement of something beautiful dropping into my life that would thrill me. Said another way, it was time for me to fly, time for me to receive. Just a peaceful feeling—and knowing. Wow. I love waking up to specific ideas or thoughts or words that I know I'm receiving from Source.

Later as I lay down for an afternoon nap, I felt into this new "you are loved" feeling that was now embedded or included in my awareness of who I am in the world. I started to daydream about sipping my latte in Rome at *the* hotel courtyard garden and this scene, which I had imagined hundreds of times, now felt very different. Now there was a deeper understanding of satisfaction and fulfillment present. It was interesting to sense something new about how I felt in this daydream scenario. There was a new clarity that this "you are loved" is the "why" and the "how" of receiving—well, what we might call outrageous shit!

Vortex Download

What's really fun and astonishing about a revelation I had during a meditation was that not only was I pitching to a famous performer their next music video but pitching to work with them on their next hit song too—giving them the theme and the inspiration and the vision for execution of the video that would promote it! Holy shit!

During and after meditation and as an extension on the theme that I am loved, I received a knowing to ask for a separate pile of money to execute the creative project that I would need for my pitch to this A-List celebrity (anonymity maintained but I knew exactly who it was because I recognized her in the visual montage I saw in my mind).

What a Ride

My six-month "energy" coaching (some might call it personal transformation coaching or life coaching) has been mind-blowing. Heart expanding. Life changing. After only one month into the program, I had leapfrogged in wisdom, joy, eagerness, and clarity beyond what countless lifetimes of simply living and figuring stuff out on my own would have taught me. The trajectory of my life path was radically accelerated beyond my wildest dreams.

I decided to search through my text history with KT for the moment I discovered the six-month coaching was available. I remember saying yes to it immediately. I also remember distinctly that when I saw how much it would cost, my inner being deliberately caused me to incorrectly calculate in my head the total cost. My inner being knew I would be a little shocked so I was guided into a "yes" in a softer way. After I texted, "I'm in!" I realized my addition error. I had only added the monthly fee by three months, not six. I quickly realized my error and felt a gulp of discomfort. But as I checked in with myself, I still felt that same certainty and eagerness of knowing I wanted the coaching. I had to chuckle when I realized my inner being was guiding me around my beliefs about money and the resistance I held. Just a few sessions in and I could easily see that I would move heaven and earth to accomplish the expansion and alignment I've experienced through working with KT. Thank you, KT, for sharing your gift with this world and with me. I will be literally eternally grateful. I would quickly trade my loft or other possessions to know what I now know. I just don't have to. I get to have it all.

It became clear to me as I focused on a theme of deliberate fun that clarity and expansion were deeply embedded in what makes me "happy." I also understand that I am eager to get on with the good stuff so it makes perfect sense that I would attract something like this intensive, focused coaching to me and my path.

Expansion is exhilarating to the soul and when I'm feeling exhilaration, *life is fun*!

Or as Esther told me in my hot seat, "I'm fun and that's all I can find!"

Take a Memo

One morning, as I moved through my breathwork session, I soared. I could feel myself escalating vibrationally and so quickly and easily right into my vortex. I was tapping into pure bliss. I knew that I was ready for my session, so I moved from the couch to the lounge room in my loft for my call with KT.

I was inspired to pick up my computer and use this time of inspiration to write. What better time to write my book than when I was in the vortex and in receptive mode. That's how I wanted this book to be written. In fact, I wanted to receive this book, not write it. As I put my laptop on my lap, the next impulse was "use the dictation feature on your phone, it will be easier to speak what you want to write into your voice memo and let your phone type the words." Whoa. I loved that I was being shown how this process could have ease connected to it. I also realized that this literally was or could be my voice or writing style as an author. It's closer to how I would tell a friend what I'm experiencing so I liked the idea of saying it instead of "writing" it.

Just Love

One day a memory surfaced that I had forgotten but that was clearly an example of when I had actually "owned the room" vibrationally. I had never recognized this before. This memory from college was a powerful example from my own life of the same energetic dynamic that was at work in a Jesus story that Esther Hicks/Abraham used to explain the power that a higher frequency has over a lower frequency.

*I want to insert here that I used to read the Bible every day and based my life on the teachings of Jesus. After watching a documentary about religions that showed how the legend of Jesus was lifted word for word from a religious leader from another culture dating a thousand years before Jesus, I became very skeptical. Then as I navigated coming out as gay to my church community, I experienced the opposite of human or divine love. I experienced brittle religious belief systems.

Over time I have softened my negative emotional response to organized religion and now fully support others who still remain in a structured belief system. Instead of looking at my beliefs or others' beliefs as right or wrong, I simply view everything now as simply preferred or not preferred. Taking the judgment of right or wrong out of the equation creates an ease or softness that is a much higher frequency than when we have assigned good or bad to people or a topic.*

Now back to the story from the Bible. Jesus healed someone who was sick with leprosy. Jesus was tuned to the powerful dominance and frequency of well-being and the sick man was tuned into the frequency of the symptoms of his disease. The man sought healing from Jesus and was healed because Jesus had owned the room vibrationally by the clarity of his understanding of well-being. To be in conversation with each other, they would need to be in the same frequency. Frequency is used here in the same way we understand how a frequency for a radio station is broadcasting content at a specific frequency. Jesus either needed to lower his vibrational frequency of thought to the sick man's lower frequency or the sick man would need to tune to the higher frequency of well-being that Jesus was tuned to. Jesus was not willing to leave his frequency of absolute health and tune down to illness. The sick man was easily inspired upward to the frequency that Jesus held fast to.

The sick man was transformed and regained his natural state of well-being. This example that Abraham sometimes references showed me I had also done this, and I could do it again. I was being shown that this was something I had already lived. This was *not* an unattainable, aspirational ideal. Was I living at the sustained, practiced level that Jesus lived? Hell no! Far from it. But I had at least experienced it once!

I was a junior in college working as a "security host" in Boston during my summer break. My role as a security host was to monitor an assigned area of the public garden within the Christian Science Center complex. This was the headquarters for the Christian Science Church. At that time, I was a hardcore Christian Scientist. I was just starting my shift and surveying the plaza where people were either cutting through to get to their neighborhood or were tourists visiting the public garden. Boston is crowded with universities and working neighborhoods and, since the plaza was in the middle of the back bay district of the city, it was constantly busy with urban pedestrians.

In the distance on the furthest edge of the flower beds was a disturbing scene. A homeless person was violently gesturing and yelling at a family trying to enjoy the flowers and reflection pool. My first thought was, "Damn, that's scary," and then it hit me. "Fuck! I'm the one that's supposed to 'handle' this!" I started to panic while at the same time slowly forcing myself to move toward the scene. I remember thinking this was not the job I wanted.

I immediately asked God to help me. I wanted a powerful Bible quote or message that would completely wipe out any doubt or fear. The words that came were simply, "Just love." I distinctly remember feeling that was way too vague and I needed something bigger that truly removed the terror I was feeling. "Just love," came again. I was running out of time and realized I had to make the best of the words that were given to me.

As I arrived, the man saw me approach and turned away from the family and pointed his anger at me. He was yelling obscenities and wildly waving his arms around. All I could think to do was stand there quietly thinking over and over, "Just love." I somehow knew my only job was to just be there as a witness to "Love." Divine Love. God. I knew I needed to not be impressed by the ugly, potentially dangerous display going on in front of me but instead to be a silent witness for good, for Love.

The man suddenly stopped and asked, "Do you respect me?"

"Yes, sir," I replied.

Right before my eyes he just melted. He went from a state of delirious anger to soft and calm. He reached out and pretended to adjust the knot of my polyester, security uniform tie and said, "You know, you look good even in this tie." I was in awe of not only the transformation but the sarcasm and irony. Here was a homeless person poking fun at the quality and bad fashion of *my* clothes. He had a point. A polyester, kelly-green blazer and a navy and green striped tie. *Not* what I was expecting from him, but wonderful. He turned and walked away in a completely different state than how it all began. What a powerful example I'd just been given.

I realized this memory was illustrating that this violent, out-of-control situation had forced me to focus because my life depended on it. In that exaggerated focus, I had been a powerful, determined witness for the well-being that I knew was present despite the chaos and anger taking place right in front of me. My conviction and trust had allowed me to vibrationally own the room. Holy shit!

I noticed that I needed this example to remind me of what's possible and that if I had done it once, I could do it again. As I examined the dynamics of my own experience, I realized that I could once again be a witness for whatever I wanted but that it had evaded me recently. The danger of my college experience had forced me to really stand strong in my knowing versus when I'd find myself in the more common situations like being annoyed at my partner when he used a condescending and dismissive tone with me. (It pushed my buttons every single time.)

Now, I was seeing that I could remain aligned. I just need to summon the conviction even when danger wasn't in play. "Just love," I would remind myself when life's little annoyances would present themselves. Ah! I'm aware in this moment to not be annoyed or frustrated, but to "just love."

News to Me

One morning after a meditation, I had an awareness that I was going to write a book. "Huh. That's news to me," I thought. I recalled being on the Pacific Coast cruise hearing from my friend Nancy that she was going to write a book. Nancy is my new dear friend that I met on my very first law of attraction cruise which sailed to Alaska. She had received an "intuitive download" a few years back that showed her the title of her future book. What's interesting to me was I had no thought in that moment of, "Oh, I want to write a book too!" Nope. I simply thought it was cool how she received that knowing. I had plenty going on in my own life and if anything, I wanted to work and promote my painting and artwork. That's it. So, it was very surprising to me that I suddenly had this awareness of a book in my future.

To my credit, I am definitely open to anything that presents itself to me at this stage in my life. That day I texted my friend Abby and told her about this book revelation. She loved the idea and suggested I work with a man whom she had worked with a few years earlier when she wrote her book. His name was Azul, and he had a gift of helping others give birth to their books. Mentoring them along their path to authorship. It sounded like a logical step, but I was still trying to process the whole idea of even writing a book. The next morning, I saw an email from Abby to Azul, introducing us to each other. Whoa, that was faster than I expected! But it felt right to allow the momentum to start. I decided to have a first zoom meeting with him and take it one step at a time.

If I'm being honest and transparent about my process and approach for writing this book, it's that my book can truly be whatever it wants to be. If anything, I'm a painter and designer, not a writer. So, it can take shape however it wants. My book is calling the shots. I'm just my book's lil' bitch (of course only in the healthiest, life-affirming way). Said another way, I'm that age-old vessel, receiving the message inside me that is ready and wanting to be told. I have an idea of what I think my book is about based on the idea that originally came to me. But I get the feeling my book will evolve into something different, something more, that surprises and delights me along the way.

FUCK. My Inner Being Is *So* Embarrassing

On Thanksgiving Day morning, I woke up abruptly with these words in my head: "Chapters are Word Sacks."

OMG are you fucking kidding me?! Noooooooooo. "Wait until I tell Nancy about this bullshit," I thought. As mentioned earlier, Nancy is my new dear friend that I met on my very first law of attraction cruise. She has also become my "book buddy" since we both are writing books. We feel like we are twins because we find ourselves navigating the same things in life ranging from leaving our corporate jobs to writing our first book.

Ok, back to the nightmare. I rolled over trying to process it. I knew I was receiving a piece of my book, but I hated it. I decided I would roll over and go back to sleep. I was never more willing to take a chance that I would forget these nuggets from heaven.

I decided that if it was meant to be, I'd remember it later when I woke up. But then this line entered my brain: "Just as Barbra Streisand was 'contractually obligated' to make Funny Lady, I'm contractually obligated to 'let my book be whatever it wants to be.'" Oh, this is fighting dirty. If my inner being is going to invoke Barbra's holy name, then fuck me! I sprang out of bed and headed to my laptop.

I was never the kid who was embarrassed by their parents, but this was in fact embarrassing. I had a slightly more sophisticated, or at the very least, less clownish vision for my voice as an author than "word sacks." If you recall, I earlier wrote that I was my book's lil' bitch. Well, I thought I was being "light" about that. I reassured you that it was in the most self-affirming way. Scratch that . . . nope. It was worse than I thought if this was the phrasing my inner being wanted me to include.

This reminded me of a morning after a particularly inspiring, deep session from my law of attraction seminar. I woke up with new names for some of the women I'd met on the cruise. We had become fast friends. At dinner the night before, the women were discussing that they didn't like the idea of keeping their married names. They had gone through difficult years and were now divorced and wanted to change their names back to their maiden names. One friend didn't like her name and had never liked it and wanted a completely new name. This was just a passing dinner conversation comment. For some reason I woke up full of names for them. Nancy would be Hyacinth Joyologist. Apparently my inner being wants my friends to be embarrassed too. Hyacinth is meant to replace "Licensed" as in "Licensed Joyologist." Since having "License" as a first name is "too far." The next friend was named Summer and her new name was "Summer Scott Claws." But bear claws not kitty claws. She was meant to be a warrior queen not a domesticated feline.

Ugh. What was happening? I knew others from my seminar were receiving divine downloads and this was what was flowing to me effortlessly? I will admit that I was finding all of this amusing and ridiculous. Looking back, it makes a little sense considering what I heard in the first session of the seminar. The idea that "fun" is the highest vibrational emotion. My inner being must have been guiding me to laughter and fun that morning. Maybe this lowbrow silliness was divine? I will admit I had previously thought of myself as funny, but this wasn't even clever. AT ALL.

The download wasn't over. Michelle was up next. She is so elegant but a true badass, so the name came "Ina FuckyouUp." These weren't even good drag queen names. At the very, very least, I liked how the names *felt* as I thought them, or let's be clear, as they were given to me. I'm not taking credit for thinking these. I like to think of myself as a little more clever than this.

Next came a fully realized drag show within the context and inspiration of Esther Hicks. As in Abraham Hicks, law of attraction fame. Seriously? *This* is my inner being download? WTAF?! For those who don't have teenage kids, that is an acronym for "What The Actual Fuck."

I lay in bed giggling but thinking you have *got* to be kidding me. But if fun is the highest vibration, at least I'm a vibrational king, top of the heap apparently.

I just always assumed I'd be allowed a shred or two of dignity but hell to the no.

Word Sack 2

Ok, inner being, I see you. Now that I've had some time to process the horror, I'm not as freaked out about how embarrassing you are. I have to reluctantly admit that this will be a fun book to write if this is what comes out. I'd like to add for the record that I have never been easily embarrassed or too concerned about what others think of me. Thank God! Of course, I'd like to be respected and admired. But I've always had a strong sense of who I am. I've always known I was a good person and felt comfortable in my own skin which has been such a valuable "knowing" to possess. I just thought my book would be witty and fun, not cringey. Oh well.

There Is No Time

One morning back at home in St. Louis, I decided it was time to get out of bed. I thought, "No time like the present." On the heels of that came the thought, "There is no time." Hmmmmm. I knew it was a message for me. I didn't fully understand what that meant for me at that point in time, but I knew that I would receive more insights on this from nonphysical.

After my shower, I sat in meditation. It came to me that I should listen to my last coaching session instead of an Abraham video or one of my favorite pieces of music that I often enjoy getting lost inside.

As I listened to the last session with KT, I started connecting so many dots. Dots from this very morning from "there is no time" and messages within my last session that I was ready to fully receive and make the mind-blowing connections that pieced together a bigger picture.

Early on in my experiment with fun, I had a realization that I came forth with an intention in this life to show that it doesn't have to take a lot of time to manifest big shit. As I sat in meditation, the words came: "I'm ready."

From my inner being I received that this is another awesome day, another awesome moment. And soon another awesome session.

Why are my sessions awesome? Because I'm awesome. And the universe is awesome!

Both are true. I eagerly anticipate and intend for my sessions with KT to be awesome. So that's the only option that can happen.

When I am in pure alignment, pure form, that really is the only thing that can happen. I eagerly anticipate this. I look forward to it. It's fun. It's awesome. So that's what the law of attraction must deliver.

One of my desires has been to own a beautiful hotel where I could enjoy all the amenities like housekeeping and a restaurant on site. The thought of waking up and taking the elevator downstairs to have a beautiful breakfast and a latte is exactly the way I would love to live. I have no idea "how" this would happen, "how" I could own a hotel, but that's not my job. My job is to desire it and then feel my way into becoming a vibrational match to it. My inner being suggested I focus on sitting and feeling all the details of owning and living in a hotel. As I've been practicing this, I noticed how different I felt from the day before to the next day's meditation!

These insights of "there is no time" and all the expansion I've felt recently added so much more dimension and richness to my inner world that as I mentally sat and basked in my future hotel courtyard sipping my latte, everything that was available to me now to feel about my life was dramatically different. "Why?" I asked KT in my next session. The answer? Because I was in receptive mode. I was (and I am) wide open for anything that is ready to come through. KT continued to explain that I wouldn't be anywhere near where I am if I came to these sessions with questions that I wanted answered. I knew that it would be the perfect thing at the perfect moment. That's a wonderful, vibrational place of no resistance, a wonderful perfection of the now moment.

Imagine if someone came to a program like this and they mapped out all six months. And they said, "On this day, I want this answer. On this day I want this answer and on this day, I want this answer." That doesn't work because your point of attraction continues to change. That was the "then" list. I've expanded. I'm on the "now" list.

It was reassuring to hear from my nonphysical self the feedback that I come to the sessions "wide open to receive whatever comes through." Whoa, that is nonresistant thought. Abraham has described nonresistant thought as a million times more powerful than thought that has doubt in it.

I started my coaching with KT in January and had a realization that the reason I'm advancing so quickly is because I'm not "learning," I'm simply remembering what I came forth already knowing.

HOLY SHIT! It's so fun when "understanding" clicks into place.

Note

1.   Jenn Beninger & Carson Cooper, "Meditation: Trusting Your Intuition," Co-Founders Genius Unlocked Coaching Institute, *YouTube*, 16 Jul. 2020.

Chapter 6

A UNICORN INSTRUCTIONAL GUIDE

MY LIFE WAS CHANGING QUICKLY AND WONDERFULLY. SO MANY new ideas and new people flowing into my life. It has been exhilarating and fascinating. Much of it is unfolding and still in front of me. I'm going to take you along for the ride and capture "the how" that is transforming my life into something wonderful and bigger and better and *faster* than I could have previously imagined.

Although I covered my early milestone experiences, this section represents what I recommend you actually *do* and the why behind it in order to transform your life. Instead of a typical list format, I've decided to weave this list within the stories that have taught me so much.

1: Meditate Every Day and Follow the Ideas That Present Themselves to You

Apparently, my inner being is my co-pilot. "Go get a latte before work" was a mental suggestion I received as I stepped into the shower one morning. "Nah. I'm good. I like being at home before my meetings start." But then I remembered Esther Hicks telling stories about getting an impulse to do something that seemed random, but she would follow through and it would lead to another impulse and then another until she was in the middle of something wonderful that she knew was the culmination of the seemingly unrelated original impulse. With that in mind, I decided to follow the suggestion to leave my loft and drive over to Comet Coffee where I could order online for an easy pick up.

As I exited the parking garage in my car, I started listening to a badass Buddhist nun who was relaying her experience with meditation. She shared the most beautiful thought that was roughly along the lines that when you frown, the cells in your body frown and when you smile, the cells in your body smile. Wow . . . I loved how profound but simple that was.

Those Buddhists! They're so good at that.

Oops. I realized I had not "segment intended," which is setting an intention of how you want to feel and how you want to experience the next thing on your schedule. An example would be as you drive to work you set an intention to have your first meeting feel efficient and harmonious. A new segment could also be when you're sitting in a room and someone enters. That changes the energy and marks a new experience from the previous one. That is deliberate creating. Setting an intention for how you want the next segment of your day to go and perhaps more importantly, how you want to feel.

So, I stopped the podcast and started affirming what I knew to be true and available to me as I drove. I knew my path was connected to the dominant wellbeing of the universe and I acknowledged the presence of wellbeing with me always. (Example: If someone cut me off in traffic, I had at least two choices before me: I could choose to be annoyed and angry or I could choose to not let whatever is going on in their life calibrate me to something different than the wellbeing I had already felt.) As I made my way to pick up my coffee order, I thought along the lines of "not only is harmony and safety available and flowing to me, but also an abundance of ideas and guidance and dollars." I can't recall the exact words, but it just flowed. I was feeling such exhilaration and appreciation that I had listened to the impulse to stop the podcast and focus on the safety of my drive because the "rampage" of abundance I had just experienced was thrilling. I'm not being dramatic. It really was pure inspiration flowing to me from Source Energy in such a powerful way.

I thought I was done and that this was definitely why I had the impulse to go get coffee so that I could receive that assurance of abundance. But as I was basking in that state of inspiration, I received an unspoken voice asking me, "Why aren't you staying at your first-choice hotel in Rome?"

Background: I had been planning a trip to Italy once it was safe to travel again after COVID and had been looking at hotels. The last thing I was expecting to hear was a question about my hotel options in Rome! I had recently landed on a ridiculously expensive hotel that was already $300 more than the previously outrageous $500 a night I had spent on my 2019 trip. My comfort zone had been around $200 a night but as my partner and I had laboriously considered all our options, I reluctantly agreed to these next-level hotels that admittedly looked to be worth every penny. Once we completed our trip in 2019, we understood that those expensive hotels had been more than a luxurious place to stay, they had been as integral to the entire trip as the gorgeous cities had been. We had the best trip of our lives. I saw both the value and the magic of a hotel like the one in Rome that had an interior courtyard with fountains and trees. I could see myself sitting and having my morning latte in absolute heaven. The other hotels were beautiful and well-designed, but they lacked an outdoor space that could come close to the Hotel de Russie. However, it was easily $1,200 PER NIGHT! There was no way I was willing to spend that much money. So instead, I selected a beautiful hotel that was still a whopping $800 per night. Now days later while driving for coffee, my inner being was asking me, "Why am I not choosing the hotel I truly desire?"

The understanding that came through clearly was this:

- My trip wasn't for another year so was I really telling the universe I couldn't receive the money needed for that hotel by then?
- Was I limiting the universe's ability to deliver the money to me in countless ways?
- Was my current paycheck the only avenue the universe had available to it?

But the biggest piece of all was this: If I wanted to move beyond my current financial status, I would need to think bigger, and then three specific words came through clearly: "If you want to be wealthy, you'll need to 'Act like it.'"

Fascinating! All at once I understood that I was being shown a practical, energetic bridge to get from where I currently was to where I desired to be financially. I could feel the power energetically of checking into that hotel and basking in that frequency of abundance and that highest level of customer service, of ease, of the quality of furnishings. I could feel the fun energy of appreciating the delicious food that was available to me there. And so, eventually, I did check in to that hotel a year later. It was a very special moment when I sat in that courtyard and ordered that greatly anticipated latte.

What I love most about this experience of driving in my car and hearing guidance about the hotel was the surprise of it. I wasn't thinking about my Rome trip. I was just flying high after experiencing an amazing river of inspiration. My nonphysical self knew what I desired, what hang-ups I held that were blocking me, and how to guide me around those limiting beliefs to what I wanted. Step by step.

I was so excited. I knew for sure that I had experienced my first "impulse," followed it, and received the breadcrumbs along that trail to the big reveal. To hear a specific sentence and message from the spiritual plane is a big fucking deal and I was on fire with enthusiasm for what I had discovered in this law of attraction stuff. It had moved from words to my own lived experience. Hell YES!

> **NOW IT'S YOUR TURN.** Listen for these impulses even if they seem as inconsequential as getting a latte before work. You will start to recognize these impulses as actual guidance once you release the strangle hold of everything always having to be logical.

2: How to Dial Up the Fun in Life through Meditation

The Alaska cruise ended in late August, and once I was unpacked and settled, I decided to schedule a beautiful trip somewhere for late November or early December. Somewhere warmer than St. Louis. After researching temperatures across the country and in multiple cities along both coasts of Mexico, I narrowed in on San Miguel, a gorgeous city a few hours from Mexico City. In San Miguel was an insanely charming Belmond hotel property. After several days of pondering the airfare and other logistics, I was definitely sold on San Miguel. But for some reason, I wasn't feeling ready to pull the trigger and book it. I decided to sleep on it and look at the hotel again the next day to see if I still loved it. Yes, it was everything I wanted. It generously checked all of the boxes of a great trip. But for some reason I couldn't commit. This was curious to me, so I asked the universe to give me an answer. Was I supposed to travel somewhere else instead? I knew the answer would come.

The next morning after meditation, I had gone into the bathroom to wash my hands and the thought occurred to me: "What about the Pacific Coast cruise?" Well, that was interesting because I'd seen the email about this seminar cruise and had already decided it was too soon after the Alaska cruise. I recalled thinking I liked the ports better than the Alaska ports, but I had already booked the Alaska cruise and was happy with my decision. The Pacific Coast cruise wasn't even an option. Or was it? As I got this answer back from the universe, I recognized it as indeed the answer to my question. I thought to myself, "Well, it would be fun. Hmmm. Maybe so!" I had been attempting to space out my fun in what I thought was a reasonable cadence, but I could feel the thrill of it and knew that this was the answer.

Now my only hesitation was to see if there was any way I could ask off another seven to ten days of vacation after having just taken two weeks off for the Alaska cruise. It was to take place in early October, and it was now early September. I decided that if it was meant to be, I'd get my manager's blessing as well as my writing partner's approval. She would have to cover for me while I was out. I was a creative director co-managing a team of writers, production artists, and art directors. Each group of brands at our agency was managed by an art creative director and a writer creative director. My background was as an art director/designer.

Soon enough I was on a zoom call with my boss and co-manager and served up my request like this: "I realize I was just on vacation, but since I still have four weeks of vacation left, would either of you mind if I take another week off in October?" I had to admit, when I presented it like that, it did seem reasonable. I had thought initially that it had to be a long shot but in reality, it wasn't an issue for anyone at all. I had been the only obstacle in my path.

Clearly the thought of going on another cruise only five weeks after my last cruise was way more fun than I had expected or planned for myself. But since I was paying attention to how I was feeling and curious about why I was feeling hesitation about moving forward with the planning of my Mexico trip, I was guided to ask the universe for clarity. And the answer came. Here was my inner being guiding me, once again, to something I didn't realize was reasonable or even possible before now. It also turns out that this was my first proof that my theory was working. By focusing first and foremost on having fun, my life would transform.

At the time I decided to book the Pacific Coast cruise in October, I knew it would be fun, but I had no idea how it would change my life. Had I known, I would have moved heaven and earth to make sure I was on that ship. Thankfully I didn't need to move heaven or earth. It was easily taken care of.

> **NOW IT'S YOUR TURN.** Add this practice of softly asking for answers to your questions and watch what happens.

3: The Magic of Working with a Mentor

Of the most impactful things I have "manifested," above all else have been my two personal coaches guiding me deeper and deeper into a life-changing understanding of who I really am.

I mentioned both of my coaches earlier in this book, but it was my first coach, KT Brady, whom I met on this second seminar cruise. Again, I first noticed her sitting in the row in front of me. It was so clear that I wanted to meet her. I saw her sitting by herself and had this unmistakable knowing that I wanted to introduce myself to her. I didn't know she was a coach or that she had profound intuitive gifts. But my inner being knew and it was the most natural thing in the world to feel the powerful resonance inside me calling us together.

Many friends that I've shared this with have looked at me like I had lost my mind. They were skeptical and could not accept anything other than our sessions were just one human giving another human advice.

I'm not here to convince anyone of anything they're not ready to accept. Either this information resonates with you, or it doesn't. Sitting behind KT in that auditorium, I felt the most heightened "yes energy" I can recall having ever experienced. I was all in. As they say, the proof is in the pudding and my life has shown me that what may not be commonly experienced by others doesn't make it untrue. There is a huge ass world out there and I was learning that I had only just scratched the surface. And besides, I was only on this ship because I had had a nearly out of body experience during meditation screaming at me ever so politely to attend that first seminar cruise. If I was going to be deterred by what is and isn't "normal," I would have turned back long ago.

> **NOW IT'S YOUR TURN.** Start noticing how you feel around people you really respect. If you find yourself thinking "I want to know what they know," recognize that as enthusiasm and entertain the idea of asking them to mentor you. Follow that calling!

4: Continue Learning from the Best: My Deep Dive into F-U-N with the Great Beyond

So here I am a month and a half after my first seminar, sitting in my second law of attraction seminar.

Esther Hicks takes the stage and makes a few announcements and then goes to the podium to invite or "tune" to collective consciousness that calls itself Abraham. Now, with the knowing of Abraham flowing through her, she kicks off the seminar with this mind-blowing nugget:

"There is nothing higher on the vibrational scale than fun. Feeling like this is the best that there is in terms of accessing all that you are, yes?"

Whoa! I couldn't believe the first words out of her mouth, through Abraham, were about this theme of fun. My new focus of fun that I had adopted as my year-long science experiment! Fun had been the last topic emphasized in the previous seminar and now it was the first words out of her mouth.

Esther moved forward to the front of the stage and scanned the audience. Each of us, with hands raised, wanted to ask collective consciousness about our individual lives. So we all raised our hands. Esther (with Abraham flowing through her) surveyed the auditorium, looking for the perfect person to kick off the seminar. Holy shit! She picked ME. What an adrenaline rush to be picked first. I felt like I was launched into the air via a huge slingshot. I popped up and made my way to the stage. THIS IS HAPPENING!

I took my seat, Esther adjusted the microphone, and we began.

I felt it was important to explain that I had been on the Alaska cruise a few months prior and how I loved that her closing message was about having fun . . . and I liked how she talked about fun being the highest vibration as she kicked off this seminar!

Esther, translating Abraham, explained to me that within that feeling of elation in fun, there's a feeling of stability, there's a feeling of anticipation, there's a feeling of lightheartedness. The thing about fun is that it is such a high vibration, there's an ease in it, a lack of resistance in it.

Fun is being in the moment because it's unfolding second by second.

Taking it further, Abraham offered a new definition of "alignment" by replacing the word "alignment" with the idea of "one who is having the most fun." This new definition of alignment is a life-changing shift in how to approach what most would say is the loftiest goal for a life lived "correctly." It presents a radical new path to success and everything we desire. In one fell swoop it strips away any formal or religious implications from a word and concept that has been held in a sacred context since the beginning of time. Wow! It was no wonder this new presentation of the word "fun" as deeply significant instead of its previously frivolous context had captured my attention in such a powerful way.

> **NOW IT'S YOUR TURN.** Learning and expanding never stops. Allow yourself to stay curious and keep your momentum going by noticing what messages or messengers are truly resonating and then take the inspired action.

5: Deliberately Trend in Fun

The conversation continued with the observation that we live much of our lives down in long valleys consumed with the chores of daily existence in contrast to the peaks available to us if we would deliberately choose to focus instead on enjoyment, recreation, and fun.

When you trend more deliberately to the upper half of the emotional scale, those higher frequency emotions become your point of attraction. Most people spend more time on their way to the higher vibrations than *at* the higher vibrations. But there is no good reason for that. The way you feel is your point of attraction, your vibrational habit. And your emotions are just a response. So, the more you trend in fun and joy and love, the more you trend in those higher vibrations. The result is more of what you want is easily allowed by you.

Abraham Hicks talks about the steps of creation in this way:

- Step one: you ask for what you desire.
- Step two: you obtain an immediate yes from Source Energy.

- Step three: You focus to become a vibrational match to what you desire. This is what Abraham calls the "allowing mode" or "receiving mode," which you accomplish through the feeling place of your focus.

NOW IT'S YOUR TURN. Be deliberate and set a daily intention to look for and *find* fun.

6: Focus On How You Feel

Still in my conversation on stage with Abraham, they offered some advice. "If we were standing in your physical shoes, what we would be focusing on is how we feel. And if you're willing to do that, then you're willing to trend into a place where more of the time you're letting in more of what you want and that allows momentum. And that is what allows greater and greater and greater degrees of attraction and amounts of attraction. Prosperity becomes more, happiness becomes more with that consistency."

So, I took having more fun to heart and especially loved the simplicity of it. I noticed it kept coming up in other people's questions throughout the seminar. When people were curious about their future and desiring guidance about their next career move, the answer was consistently "have fun" because the answers will be allowed within this frequency of fun.

Because fun is the state of allowing. And everything else is already taken care of because you did step one (asking), and Source is doing step two (giving), and if you're having fun, you're doing step three (allowing). So, everything's in alignment.

I love that, because typically as humans there's a lot of logistical details that we are used to taking care of.

Society has warned us to make sure we are not putting too much fun into the equation. But most people don't get it. Most people would rather hear you say I will strive for determination, and I will focus myself and sacrifice myself into accomplishment.

And when you throw fun into that equation, it's too frivolous for them, they don't get it . . . but fun *is* it! Fun and love and joy and appreciation. Those are the emotions that are the strongest indicators of your most allowance.

I realize how limited my idea of fun was. At that time, I simply planned more travel to add more fun into my twelve-month experiment. Abraham liked my experiment idea but encouraged me to go further. They explained that it's nice to have an intention about something and to plan for those big events. But when they were talking about alignment or fun, alignment meaning the awareness of an emotion that feels good while you're experiencing it, they were talking about those moment to moment to moment-to-moment kinds of fun. Abraham was encouraging feeling and finding the fun in every moment-by-moment situation.

> **NOW IT'S YOUR TURN.** When you're in a moment of fun, pause and notice how you feel and say, "I want more of this feeling."

7: Expect the Unexpected

One of my absolute favorite parts of fun is that element of surprise. All the planning in the world doesn't produce the magic that arises when we are fully present in this "now" moment that is unfolding. My ability to inhabit this energetic frequency of fun allows me to match up to all of the cooperative components around me that are as fun as the fun I'm feeling. This is the law of attraction. And when you have been deliberate in deciding how you want to feel instead of letting the conditions outside of you determine how you feel, that is when you are truly free. Once you've been practicing this for a sustained amount of time, you gain a momentum within this higher frequency of emotion—momentum at the same frequency of abundance and well-being. You are "trending" and now you are in control of what comes. More fun, more clarity, more abundance, more well-being, more joy, more opportunities to feel good.

It is so thrilling to receive an impulse or idea that feels like it came out of nowhere. It didn't come out of nowhere; it's been trending for some time so that there is now momentum animating your daily experience. When you foster an atmosphere of feeling good, of alignment, of fun and lightheartedness, these are some of the best parts of this frequency of fun. It's gotten to the point where I am so used to feeling great joy and inspiration that I reach for it until I find it. And not only every morning but continuously throughout the day.

To be living my experiment of fun and to now be sitting on stage and having a master class deep dive on this very topic of fun with Esther and Abraham was everything I had hoped it would be. This ended up being a thirty-minute discussion on the nuances of "fun" and was beautiful evidence of the law of attraction at work. Think about it! I had decided to write a book about the powerful transformation of fun and who was I discussing fun with? Esther and Abraham . . . Holy shit! This illustrates in such a dramatic way that whatever you think about is for sure attracted into your experience. THIS is my kind of fun!

> **NOW IT'S YOUR TURN.** Decide today that you will live your life in an expectation of surprise and delight as your new normal.

8: Live Like You're Always on Vacation

Next Abraham shifted into a new thread of advice.

> [These rich and satisfying results caused by fun were] what we wish for you in all times not just while on vacation. We want that to be your attitude because the universe is yielding to you. When you understand how it all works and you stop feeling guilty, you're having fun instead of sacrificing and then you are operating from the upper half of the emotional scale most of the time.
>
> Since you're trending that way, things get better and better and better so that things that seem sort of inconsequential but aren't begin piling up in lovely ways until there can be just a stream of events that happen where you know you are so blessed. When you're steady and trending in the upper half of the emotional scale, the clarity about what to do next occurs to you so that you're right on point.[1]

I had used the expression "pulling the trigger" when I had been planning that wonderful trip to Mexico. Abraham explained that often when you arrive at the point in time where you make a decision, the clarity you feel can be immediate because you have been trending on a topic and even how you want to feel within that topic. You don't want to make a decision just because it's time to make the decision. Esther told me a new story that is now one of my favorites. It was about her making big, important decisions that most people would contemplate over a long period of time. But Esther could feel such powerful resonance that she would move right into action.

> **NOW IT'S YOUR TURN.** Start today and live as if you are always on vacation. Let life feel light and allow life's decisions to feel relaxed and easy.

9: Have Fun to Bring Solutions

Esther continues by explaining that if she had discussed buying a new home with some of the people that were close to her, they would have wanted her to be reasonable. She joked that they should be way past expecting that from her by now. Because reasonable usually means considering the pros and the cons, the pluses and the minuses. And in that process, you shoot all the good trending in the foot. It stops the momentum when you weigh the pros and the cons. You're slowing your momentum way down and your fun factor goes out the window. When you're aligned and fun is something that has not only momentum but also a very strong intention, you will find fun everywhere you go and fun in every moment. Esther playfully explained that if there were a camera on her all of the time, they would've locked her up as she talked out loud to the nonphysical friends she has who she knows are setting up endless things to surprise and delight her. She knows that sounds crazy and she knows, in human standards, it's certainly not normal to be enjoying life as much as she does.

I interjected that I had noticed I was guided around my resistance by my inner being who knows what I want and who knows the resistance I have on any subject. I was aware of the Pacific cruise but had already said no to it. But since I asked for clarity, I received the answer. I mentioned that I had really loved learning that we want to avoid being in problem solving mode because then we are taken out of the receiving mode. As I felt the enthusiasm to say yes to this second cruise, I felt a flood of logistical "problems" that I would need to solve. I refused to entertain any of the problems and allowed myself to stay in the "why" it felt good to say yes to the cruise.

Abraham responded that my use of the phrase "problem solving" was eliciting something from them that they had never said before. They explained that the words "problem solving" don't go together because the problem and the solution are two entirely different vibrations. That's what's been wrong with that expression all along. They explained that when you're in the problem-solving mode, you're in the asking mode. But if you're in the fun mode, you're in the solution mode. If you're in the fun mode, you're in the answer mode which is the receptive mode. "If you're in the fun mode, you're in the letting it in mode." I loved hearing yet another important reason why FUN is so powerful!

I explained that was why the experiment of applying fun really jumped out at me and resonated within me in such a powerful way.

> **NOW IT'S YOUR TURN.** Avoid giving audience to the objections and concerns that come racing in as a new idea is hatched within you. Don't leave your enthusiasm. Stay in the receiving mode.

10: Look for "What's Next?" to Be Available Now

I continued that I had recently become aware that I had a "what's next" in my career. I had been watching a seminar video from the previous cruise where a mom was talking about raising children (my coach Liz!). As they were growing up, this mother was feeling sad about that chapter ending. Abraham explained to her in that discussion that she had absolutely been putting plenty of "what's next" into her vortex.

When I first heard this mother's situation, I had thought, "This doesn't apply to me. I'm not interested in having more children." I was about to fast forward through the video, but then as I heard the discussion, I suddenly felt inside me an exciting realization that I had a what's next too. I thought I was going to stay in my current corporate position where I was beautifully set up in a feathered nest. But I realized—wait, this isn't the freedom I truly desire. I knew there was always more freedom available to me.

Abraham explained that my realization was hitting on something important but that it could be explained better regarding how impactful desiring "more" is to our life experience, to our creation, to our expansion. This desire for more is how we define what we prefer. We've done so much of that through living, that there is this vibrational reality that is just beginning to unfold with our conscious attention to it.

Abraham introduced an example of a seed you plant in the ground. They emphasized that there is intentionality in it. There is intentionality in tending to it. It's going to become something more than a seed in the ground. It's going to be a plant, and it's going to produce food. Because it has so much life force and intentionality already in it, you are not required to focus intently on that seed.

There is also a certain expectation of the seed doing what it is meant to do and so we want to feel that way about the seeds that are calling us. Our "what's next" seeds are in the state of becoming; so, in essence, they are real and in present tense. A baby that is in the womb is present tense even though it hasn't left its interior world for the exterior world.

I started to grasp what Abraham was telling me. There is power in understanding that what you call your future state, your what's next, is actually present tense. It may seem like a subtle distinction, but it brings what you desire more into the now versus unintentionally holding it out and away from you and stuck in the future. And so, the "what's next" takes on a new understanding because it's not "next," it's "now" more realized. It's already underway. It's real, it is happening, and that's different than "future state." It's something that is real and it's becoming but there's no rush for it to make its entrance in a physical way into my experience until I am really ready to receive it fully.

Because when something comes at the right time and right place, that means I am a cooperative component to it and its readiness for me. Abraham was describing what creation was in a new way. Creation is not the moment of birth. That's only one moment in the creation. The moment and act of conception is a gigantic moment of the creation process!

There's so much that has been going on behind the scenes. So, the more fun, alignment, inspiration, curiosity you are having, the less it's behind the scenes. The more you have a sense or awareness of it, when a piece of it shows up, you recognize it. Like when I decided that I wanted to go on that cruise, it wasn't in my plan at all.

> **NOW IT'S YOUR TURN.** Choose to meditate and find your alignment each morning. By doing this, you are tending to your point of attraction. This regular practice builds positive momentum and creates the vibrational environment that ushers in thriving. Now you have access to what you previously thought was your future state.

11: Set an Intention to Rendezvous with Fun

Esther shared a story about a high-rise condominium she found in San Antonio. I loved the synchronicity of how it naturally unfolded as a result of her living a life of alignment and from the momentum of her intention to rendezvous with fun. This new home was not in her plan.

Esther joked about her daughter locking her up because of the irrational decisions she continued to make about things. Her daughter asked her how long she had been thinking about purchasing this condominium.

Esther admitted that she had the first thought yesterday. Her daughter asked if she was sure it was what she wanted.

"Yes, I can't live without it," Esther responded.

This response in particular made me laugh out loud on stage. I could totally relate to that feeling of clarity and enthusiasm that happens when something you discover thrills you. Esther could feel that it fit everything she cared about. Her daughter was incredulous because Esther had only known about the condo since the day before.

Esther brilliantly pointed out that the condo only came out where she could mentally play with it yesterday, but it had been in the works for a very long time. It's a high-rise building in a part of San Antonio with incredible views and there are people on staff all around her that want to do nice things for her.

She's not going to be there very much but it's sure fun when she's there to have those experiences. Esther explained that she may not have been thinking of the answer per se, but she had been thinking about multiple questions. Her life was organically presenting questions to her like the following:

- How can I have more fun?
- How can I have more ease?
- Where can I find more excellent restaurants?
- Where are there more walking trails?
- Where can I live where the weather is consistently pleasant?
- How can I be closer to where my office and staff are?
- How can I collaborate more with them?

There were hundreds and hundreds of questions that were queued up for her. And then the one day she was in San Antonio flying through on her way from a birthday trip with her daughter, someone was talking about this particular building.

Esther wasn't aware of this building and asked her friend to tell her more about it.

She learned it was in a part of town she really liked and then her friend pulled up pictures of it online. Esther loved it and wondered if she could get an appointment to see it. Yep.

Could she get inside the unit that was available? Yep. Next, she was inside the unit.

After explaining the features of the property, the real estate agent asked Esther how she felt about the unit.

"I'll take it," she responded.

> **NOW IT'S YOUR TURN.** Practice being spontaneous and loose. Allow yourself to create a list of what you love that is inspired from today, not from five years ago.

12: Trust Your Inner Enthusiasm

As the story continued, Abraham explained that to a lot of people, the freedom to make a decision that quickly was crazy! Most would insist that you must torture yourself much longer on any decision that you make. But that isn't how the universe works!

The universe knows who we are. The universe knows who Esther is and what she wants.

The universe knows every facet and factor of our life experience and is willing to guide us to optimum experiences, moment after moment after moment. And in the moment Esther has had enough of this high-rise condo, the universe will bring her someone who passionately wants it and who will pay her more for it than what she paid.

Esther knows that nothing is permanent. Everything is passing through our experience for our surprise and pleasure and delight, but most of us don't know that. We've been trained into an attitude of struggle and sacrifice.

Abraham explained to me that that's just not normal. It's maybe the way most humans live, but it's not the way the laws of the universe work. It's not the way the power of the seed in the ground works. Everything operates by the path of least resistance or path of most allowance. And allowance of what? Allowance of alignment and connection and cooperation and joy and power and more.

NOW IT'S YOUR TURN. Notice when you're feeling playful and joyful. This is you in the frequency of fun which is the frequency of allowance.

13: Stop Expecting Others to Know What's Best for You . . . Only You Know!

This on-stage discussion continued as I interjected that my new motto was going to be Esther's feeling about her new condo: "I can't live without it."

Abraham responded that we only think or say "I can't live without that" when we truly feel that way because there are many things that are not right now for us. But when it feels like that, "pull the trigger" and don't let someone who doesn't understand you—who hasn't been the creator of your vortex with you, who hasn't walked every step of your life with you, who doesn't really know who you were the day you were born—tell you what's right for you. No one else can know what's right for you or when it's right for you. Only you know!

I was starting to realize that this on-stage discussion felt like it was lasting forever. I loved how much time they were spending with me in this discussion.

Abraham continued by explaining that your inner being knows every single thing that matters and cares more deeply, more completely, more clearly, more broadly than they can even explain to us.

But there's a worthiness issue with most people. Most people can't quite let themselves go there. And here's why.

Many of us don't allow ourselves to go with the flow of Source's understanding of who we are and what we want and what we're ready for. Instead of calibrating on a regular basis with nonphysical energy, we've been calibrating to other humans.

What do you think? What do you think I should do? But when you ask somebody else what they think you should do, they think you should do what's best for them.

Every single time. They don't mean to be that way. Other humans will want you to live in their neighborhood so that you are within car borrowing distance and so on.

NOW IT'S YOUR TURN. Unsubscribe from external opinions.

14: Improve Your Ability to Let in What You Desire

Abraham paused and gave me a chance to continue. I returned to my enthusiasm of that moment when I realized I had a "what's next" that I had not previously felt inside me. I had felt so content and satisfied and tickled with my corporate job that it felt like a major surprise when I realized I wanted something else, something even better. I had felt it vibrationally.

"What's next" sounds future tense. And from the vortex or vibrational point of view, it's present tense. Everything starts as an idea, a thought, a feeling before it becomes physical. So, it is in a mental state of existing. It still is real, it exists, just not physically yet. From the "what I'm ready to let in" point of view, it's future tense. But for *what's ready* to be let in, it's present tense.

What am I ready for next?

What am I most ready for?

Because when I say, "what's next," it makes it sound like it's not ready, but it is.

It's my readiness that Abraham is talking about. Not the job, not the fortune, not the relationship, not the fun, not the cruise. Those things are already accomplished and ready for me. It's more about am I ready for it? Am I a vibrational match to it?

Through this discussion with Abraham, I discovered that the more fun I have, the more I'm up for what's ready for me.

Wow, don't you love that?!

Abraham was basically telling me that my next readiness is vastly improved with my intention for fun. That my fun has prepared me for what's been ready for me that I didn't even know I was ready for.

It isn't just fun the day you think of the condominium and get it.

It's been fun every day before that for different reasons. That's not what caused the fun. That's just part of the ongoing fun.

That's just a culminating, strong focal point. That is evidence of all the fun that Esther has been having every step of the way. The condominium is not the reason for all the fun. It's extremely satisfying because satisfaction comes only from one place, and that's from moving in the direction of the desire you've been asking for.

Our on-stage discussion ended with Abraham telling me this: "We are appreciative that you kicked us off in this powerful way . . . really good, really good!"

> **NOW IT'S YOUR TURN.** Shift your awareness to the reality that what you want is already accomplished. Instead, it's your readiness to be a vibrational match to it that needs your focus and attention.

15: Start Your Own Game of Creation: Shirtless Men and Butterflies

Several months after that seminar discussion with Abraham, I learned that KT offered private coaching, which started the first week of January in 2022. Early on a game of creation was introduced. I was invited to choose two objects to look for as a fun game that demonstrated how manifestation and deliberate creation work. Specifically, what did I want to look for and see over the next week as evidence of law of attraction and focus? Not totally understanding the game, I chose "hotel suites." But it wasn't "what did I want to manifest as an experience," rather it was "what did I want to see 'show up' visually on my path over the next week." Oh. Well duh, shirtless men were my first answer. Then my second choice of what to see crossing my path. Hmmm . . . butterflies! Because they are fun ways to have the universe say, "Hello, we see you."

The next day I was talking on the phone with KT (as KT the person not the translator of my inner being). While we were talking, I received a text from Abby, the friend I met up with in Arizona. Out of the blue she sent me a photo from her trip to Las Vegas where she had stayed at the Bellagio. The photo she sent was her looking up at a beautiful installation of butterfly sculptures suspended from the ceiling. Wow! It was starting! During the same phone call, I received a text from a coworker whom I was to have a status meeting with. When I opened her text, she had sent me a gif of a shirtless guy jogging down a beach. It was something we had decided ages ago as our humorous way of telling each other it was time for our meeting when the other was late. I'd totally forgotten about our silly system. OK . . . This is fun! Hell yes to butterflies and shirtless men!

The next morning, I received a text from KT: "Make-up session is today!!!"

Instead of our usual morning time, the guidance coming to KT from nonphysical in a very strong way was to have the session later in the day.

Once my morning work meetings were complete, I decided to get out of my loft and get out in the world. I needed to let the world rendezvous with me since nonphysical wanted the session to happen later in the day, I figured something cool was going to happen that we would then discuss in the session.

NOW IT'S YOUR TURN. Make sure you are getting out into the world and allowing the universe to rendezvous with you.

16: Trusting "Big You" to Guide "Little You"

I headed out of my building and decided to take a walk and listen to my favorite playlist. I was ready to be guided to whatever experience or person was waiting for me. It was such a happy, expectant feeling to know something was about to go down even if I had no idea what it was yet. As I walked downtown, I could feel a distinct intuition guiding me to where to walk. It was a subtle guidance but clear and easy to follow. We easily make decisions about which way we want to head as we start a walk and don't think anything of it. This time I was listening and aware of that intuition to go this or that direction. But mostly I was just happy taking my walk while I listened to my music.

I found myself heading east on the main street of downtown when suddenly I got an impulse to take an abrupt right and cross the street so I could head south down a side street. Ok, sure . . . why not? As I walked south two blocks, I ran into the library. Installed on the side of their building was a huge aluminum sculpture of a human face with the most elaborate explosion of butterflies I've ever seen in my life. OMG! I couldn't believe it. If I had walked a half block either direction, I would not have encountered this sculpture.

I *loved* the precision of the guidance to suddenly turn right and that I easily heard it and responded without knowing why. I also *loved* the abundance of the butterflies. This wasn't one or two butterflies but easily seventy butterflies emerging from the top of the sculpture's head. And if this weren't enough, as I had stopped to take in the scene, the song lyrics playing in my AirPods were "butterflies all having fun, you know what I mean . . . this old world is a new world and a bold world for me." I mean, come on! The ability of the universe to line up so many details simply to thrill us is mind blowing. The song was "Feeling Good" by Nina Simone. I will never forget this moment. I took a few photos and continued my walk.

I looked up through the trees at the sky as I walked through a small park across from the library. I have never felt such a high note of elation before.

To feel the precision of the, "No . . . go down this side street. Okay." And then to realize as I got there that these butterflies were only on this one spot . . . on this end of the street. It was just a really beautiful experience.

When I got that very specific impulse, turn right, right here, I didn't ask why. I just turned right. That's a perfect example of me following me. And listening to my impulses. And not wondering, "Well what's it going to be?" Or "why?" Thankfully I didn't say why. I just followed and "ta-da."

It was huge. It was this gigantic display of butterflies. It was perfect. It was a wow . . . it was a WOW!

Finally, the time came to have my session with KT and I couldn't wait to discuss what had happened with my inner being. As the session began, I described step by step what I had experienced from my perspective. My inner being reminded me that it was only the first twenty-four hours of my fun exercise with the law of attraction and yet I had had such precision as I followed my own impulse. And then the abundance of the butterflies! That's how much detail the universe has paid attention to every moment of my life. Knowing exactly where I was, exactly what I was doing. And they really wanted to stress that it was me who knows. It wasn't some mystical God, or even "all that is" or "focused consciousness." No! They wanted me to start accepting and realizing that it simply boiled down to me.

NOW IT'S YOUR TURN. Begin accepting that you can trust yourself to deliver!

17: Start Expecting More of You to Show Up

It's Me talking to me. And it's the Me that is so in tune with every detail, every moment, every tiniest of thoughts, or phrases, of my eternal experience, that everything is documented. Because it's always been Me talking to me. In my session with KT, my inner being asked me to imagine my nonphysical self, the biggest part of me, as me but without resistance, without the physical body. I was now in a new place where I could start grasping what that feels like.

That's who has been guiding me my entire existence. It has always been me.

As my session continued, my inner being gave me more detail about what I often refer to as "the fullness of me" and how that fullness specifically translates into my physical experience. They explained that because I am so powerful or in tune or "awesome in every way" (as KT loves to say), I simply chose to create a human body and go play for a while and experience all kinds of things. And, from that, I was going to expand and grow, and I would become more. And I'm going to help my beautiful planet become more. But in all these cases, it's always me doing it. "Have you ever truly thought about that?" they asked. Abraham has talked about how they taste the ice cream through you. It's nonphysical you and the physical extension of you. They (my inner being and any additional nonphysical consciousness present) really wanted to bring this concept of this blending in the human form to a deeper place of knowing. They told me that they were looking and scanning through billions of scenarios for the perfect human example that would mean the most to me.

"Let's see how this one lands. How much do you know about plants?" they said.

They used an example of an aloe vera plant because you can take a piece of it and put it somewhere else, and it will grow. It is still the same plant, is still a part of that same plant, and has come from that original aloe vera plant.

That's me in physical form. I'm the part of the plant that was taken off the aloe vera plant and put here.

Scanning again for another example, they invited me to think about when cells divide and multiply themselves. They are still cells, and they are part of the same mechanism. "What if when you're first being formed, the cells that are specifically heart cells start beating *before* they all find each other and become the human heart? It's still a part of the physical body. They are simply unique cells.

That's how you are. You're still nonphysical. You're a unique human in the entire universal expression of life, and the entire human race realm. You're that specific; you're that detailed. But you're still part of the whole at the exact same time. So you're still nonphysical, and there's a part of you that is Reid Thompson. Now you're getting there. You are nonphysical. And a part of you started beating as though it were a 'heart cell' and emerged into a physical form. You're still the big picture. You simply have part of your focus into being a heart cell, a.k.a. being Reid Thompson."

Wow. I was so fascinated and appreciative of this bigger perspective that my inner being knew I was ready to receive.

This made me think of the analogy of the ocean. It's a huge ocean but it is still comprised of countless individual droplets of water.

The reason they liked the heart cell example better was because you can take a cup of water out of the ocean and you can take it far, far away. The fact that you can separate them makes it a less accurate example. But if you were to take your heart cells out, that wouldn't work. You can't separate the integral heart cells from the functioning wholeness of the body.

"And Reid Thompson could not exist without the whole. It's another proof you can never be separated from who you really are. You are the bigger part. There's just a tiny part of your focus here in your physical form."

Wow again.

They asked me to keep thinking about this and reminded me that the next two months were going to "blow blow blow blow blow your mind." These sessions would be a deeper, richer, in-depth conversation of the leading edge than has ever been had.

> **NOW IT'S YOUR TURN.** As you move through your day, actively acknowledge and stay in an awareness that you are connected to the intelligence and creation power of the universe.

18: Own Your Power

They explained that these sessions were helping me continue my momentum forward of me truly knowing myself as nonphysical energy.

"You truly are Source or God energy. You are the *whole* shebang. And there's a part of that energy focused into Reid Thompson. That's how you're so powerful. That's why your focus is so powerful. When you get in tune with the truth of who you are, that's how everything is at your fingertips, because you *are* everything."

I could feel the thrill of what they explained and what it meant and the implications of this on my life as "Reid." I told them that I had felt this same perspective that morning in a new, clearer, natural way than ever before as I looked out my window in St. Louis, knowing I was Source Energy *and* fully blended with physical Reid. It was really special.

"Yes, it was amazing, and it was felt by all of us," they added.

What a thrilling day this had turned into!

"That's where you are. Because now your new expanded norm is becoming your norm."

And to think that this all started from meditating and realizing that I could *feel* and *be* instead of just thinking. I grew in this new awareness and the desire to prioritize my feelings by asking myself, "What's the most enjoyable way to experience my eternal journey?"

They pointed out that I was at the place where it had moved from being a concept to something that I could feel the actual reality of. The feeling and point of attraction space of it. From it being a belief into a "knowing" and or "being."

As this session began to wrap up, they told me, "We are so enjoying your journey. We are so enjoying chatting with you. And listen to this over and over. If you fancy even just listening to it one time, it will really remind you of that energy that you're in. And that new awareness, that new certainty, that new knowingness that you have become. You're no longer seeking it; you've become it. And we can even go a step further and say, well, did you become it? Or did you let yourself be it? Because you're already all that is! There's so much more. There are so many ways to talk about the magnitude of the now."

Ohhhh, the magnitude of the now! I remember when they first used those words and how I couldn't wrap my brain around "now" feeling very big or significant compared to the future I was able to imagine. I was glad they said that because I remembered cherishing, relaxing, and expanding into that idea of the magnitude of the now. And finally, that happened that morning and just now. With that feeling of being fully blended with nonphysical as I looked out my window at the St. Louis cityscape.

They agreed and explained that I had clearly heard that truth. And that it was a perfect example of the fact that I really have always been the one who created these sessions. I had heard the impulse. I had heard the vibrational feed that was coming through . . . all pointing to the truth of who I really am.

> **NOW IT'S YOUR TURN.** Take time each morning to just *feel* and just *be* instead of thinking. Bask in this feeling place that at this very moment you are Source Energy fully blended with the physical you.

19: Invest in Yourself: Your Expansion Is Worth More than What You Spend on a Car

The session ended and I sat there appreciating the value of doing this kind of self-expanding work. I can't imagine my life without these kinds of breakthroughs. I will forever be an advocate for others to invest in themselves through "self-improvement" or "inner work."

My life is forever changed as a result of even one of these sessions let alone the momentum of two sessions a week for six months!

(Spoiler alert: I continued beyond the six months and have no intention of stopping!)

> **NOW IT'S YOUR TURN.** Ask the universe, your divine team, your inner being, to show you new ways to expand. Ask your inner being to introduce you to a mentor or energy coach that would open you up to the version of this life that you intended to live when you decided to come forth. Then release it and joyously live your life and let it unfold naturally.

21: Stop Looking

It was a beautiful day in St. Louis. Seventy degrees, sunny, perfect! I had lunch with my two daughters and then headed to my beloved Forest Park to bask in the elation I always feel and get some cardio in as well. As I listened to my music, I enjoyed the beautiful temperatures and took in all the inspiring, happy lyrics of my music. I turned the corner on my path, and what did I see? A shirtless man! I forgot about my fun little game, but there he is.

One important dynamic I learned from previous sessions was that when I was looking for butterflies or shirtless men, it was in a different energy. My only job was to ask or think of what I wanted to see and then just live my life. Nonphysical pointed out that when I discovered the huge butterfly sculpture, I hadn't been looking for it. I was just on my walk and living my life.

So, I recognized that when I saw this shirtless guy, I wasn't expecting it. Excellent. I continued along my path in the park. Oh snap. There's a second shirtless guy in a boat with his friends. As I finished my walk, I tallied eight shirtless men and one white butterfly that had flown right in front of me. Life was good.

I got in my car to head home. As I was about to turn and take the highway home, I got the impulse to take a different route instead. It was a slower way home, but without hesitation I adopted this new route and merged into the left lane to head east. As I fully arrived in the left lane, a dense cloud of monarch butterflies flew into my lane and engulfed my car. Holy shit! I loved this so much. Again, with the effortless receiving of guidance, the natural following of the guidance and then boom. Here's what's fun: if I had not merged into that left lane at that exact moment, I would have encountered maybe one or two butterflies. I loved not only the precision but the abundance that resulted. A large cloud of monarch fucking butterflies! I was very much into the abundance of this experience. And the ease. I wasn't trying to accomplish anything. I wasn't looking for butterflies. I was living my life joyfully and was effortlessly guided to abundance. AND the song on the radio was "I Saw You Coming" by Bob Moses. Yes, my non-physical self saw me and knew me. And it knows where I'm going at all times and delivers wonderful abundance, joy, surprise, and delight.

I really love knowing that I don't have to "look" for anything or "effort" anything. I just get to live my life of fun. I'm not going to *miss* anything. It's done. Party on!

NOW IT'S YOUR TURN. Ask for or think of what you want to see show up on your path but pick two things that you don't have any attachments to. Don't pick something "big" like money. Choose something specific like yellow shirts or elephants and then just live your life.

Note

1. Abraham Hicks, Pacific Coastal Law of Attraction Cruise seminar, 11–19 Oct. 2021.

Chapter 7

MY UNICORN BIRTH

The Shedding of My Old Life

THIS SECTION IS ABOUT IDENTIFYING THE BELIEF SYSTEMS THAT are holding us back from living the life we desire. I go into significant detail about the ending of my relationship because it illuminated so many beliefs I was carrying around that were not aligned with what I ultimately desired.

I didn't even realize which belief systems I was holding onto until they were staring me in the face. In one of my most profound sessions with KT, my inner being gave me a slightly uncomfortable insight: "You're addicted to knowing the path. You want to know ten steps out in front of you what is going to happen. You want to check and recheck all ten steps." That's a belief system of needing to cling to what is known versus enjoying one step at a time. Or the need to know how something will show up versus embracing and relaxing into the essence of what I desire and then letting that something show up in any form. Being truly open to any path. My job is to identify what I desire; the "how" is not my job. That is accomplished by the infinite resources of the universe by my nonphysical self.

For example, I want a relationship that feels easy and comfortable. That feels like home but is also an adventure. That desire of mine could have come to me in countless ways but I was so focused on improving my then-current relationship, it never occurred to me that a path to the relationship I desired might be with an entirely different person. I wasn't even open to the idea that what I desired could show up in the form of me being alone or in a completely different situation.

Life Can Change on a Dime

One moment I was in a seminar in a forever relationship, and the next moment I wasn't. This was my third seminar cruise I had attended. A woman in the hotseat relayed that her mother had committed suicide when she was young. She felt abandoned. No goodbye message or checking in with her before she left her daughter behind. To add insult to injury, it was on her twenty-first birthday. That's a lot to process for anyone. After the woman had finished setting up some of her biographical details, Abraham had a bold perspective to help this woman reframe her entire life. Abraham told this woman that her mother was pretty much just living her independent life. She hadn't done anything *to* her. The woman wasn't a victim. It was a radical reframing of what we would normally call a horrific event. Now it was reframed as everyone is living their lives how ever they choose. Her mother wasn't supposed to be a stand-in for her daughter's inner being, and all of us listening could feel this daughter reframe her entire perspective and release the heavy burden of that profound hurt. This woman also had children and Abraham explained that when she feels concern for her children, she isn't seeing her children as their inner beings see them.

This jumped out at me in a big way. I realized in that moment that I had been concerned for my partner and by taking on that perspective of concern, I was part of the problem. I realized that since I wasn't my partner's inner being, I wasn't responsible for his happiness. My first relationship was with myself. Was I calibrating unintentionally to him and not even realizing it? Was I trying to juggle both of our states of happiness? I had been unaware that I was factoring him too much into the equation when I calculated what makes me happy. Whoa! I realized in that moment that I had been taking on a misplaced sense of responsibility for his happiness, and at my own expense.

A New Equation

What did I want? If I was truly the only one in the equation, what would I choose? I instantly realized that I wasn't willing to leave the relationship because I have always been horrified by the thought of hurting the people I love. I also realized in that moment that I can't really hurt him by choosing *my* path to happiness. I had always believed that we would work it out and fine tune anything that was out of sync. I understood for the first time that my only responsibility was to feel into my truth and walk in that direction. I could see there were two paths for us as a couple: work with a couple's therapist or leave the relationship. It was horrifyingly clear that my truth was to leave the relationship. My stomach turned upside down. I assumed we would get married. I had envisioned a ridiculously beautiful wedding in Capri or Ravello Italy. This revelation felt shocking.

But it also felt true.

I had been calling clarity and expansion into my life for months in so many areas and I knew this was exactly that: new clarity. The other revelations I had previously experienced from doing this inner work felt exhilarating and beautiful, but this was nauseating and terrifying. I learned that I had been so focused on the path of us always being together as a couple that I had not allowed the possibility of moving toward a larger life of freedom and ease other than this one path. There are so many paths to our ever-expanding life of abundance and joy. I learned that I needed to focus only on how I want to feel and not focus on the "how" it will come.

Marilyn Monroe is attributed to having said, "I believe that everything happens for a reason. People change so that you can learn to let go, things go wrong so that you appreciate them when they're right, you believe lies so you eventually learn to trust no one but yourself, and sometimes good things fall apart so better things can fall together."[1]

Releasing Old Patterns

I could feel my old pattern of needing to be understood and seen as the good guy. Never the bad guy. It had always been important to me that I did the right thing. But I realized that I couldn't factor into my equation what my partner wanted or what he thought was right for me. I knew at my core that it would be ridiculous to check with him to see if he agreed with my clarity. That would be unreasonable and illogical. I knew I had way more than just a good idea of what I wanted. I had received stunning clarity from my nonphysical self.

Nothing is going wrong here. Nobody has to "get me."

Sitting in the seminar with this stunning revelation, I took notes that were exactly what I needed to navigate the dreaded conversation. I captured the key ideas that were really resonating with me:

- "This is not a protest of our relationship but me advocating for me and following my clarity at any cost."
- "Nothing's going wrong here."
- "It's not my job for others to know what I know."
- "Your inner being will call you beyond your comfort zone."

- "You are so free, you can choose bondage."
- "Look for happiness where it IS, not where it was." (gulp!)
- "Perfection = change."
- "Fear of failure isn't law of attraction."
- "Satisfaction is moving in the direction of what is desired."

The seminar continued as a man took the stage for his hot seat question-and-answer style discussion. His subject was relationships. He described his recent break up. He said that he and his girlfriend were known as the life of the party. They would go to a bar in funny costumes, and everyone would quickly gather around them and join in. Now that he was single, he was finding it hard to let go. He couldn't shake the feelings of sadness and loss.

In response, Abraham offered that instead of him thinking that they, as a couple, were the life of the party, that instead he should adopt a new mantra: "I'm the party" and "my alignment allows the party." He couldn't look to someone else to feel good or to find alignment. The good-feeling fun always has to be found between your nonphysical self and your physically focused self . . . you and You. Abraham offered that this man had been looking for fun where it was, not where it *is*. This discussion resonated with me as well.

The Relationship Session

I went straight from the seminar to my weekly session with KT who was also attending the seminar that week. We found a reasonably quiet spot on the ship and settled in. She tuned to my nonphysical self and off we went. As the conversation progressed, I asked about my relationship and what had been revealed to me as my path. I had clarity but didn't like that I felt terrified and nauseous.

In actuality, the session had started the first day of the cruise when I ran into KT in the main cafeteria. KT was voicing my inner being and suddenly asked, "What are you going to do about the vibrational difference between you and your partner?"

Why do you ask? I thought. I was caught off guard and immediately felt terror.

As we sat down to eat a snack, I anxiously responded that I guess I would listen and follow whatever guidance came through. This thread of the conversation did not continue and although it changed direction, the seed had been planted. Or "the bomb had been dropped" feels way more accurate.

So, in our official session I wanted to ask about that bombshell of a question that they had initiated.

My inner being suggested that perhaps I already knew the answer to their question but was looking for affirmations.

But in my mind, I was way down the path of what I thought the solution was, which was me striving to be more unconditional and not waiting for outside conditions to change in order for me to be really clear and steady in my own vibration. If I was aligned, the things that frustrated me about my partner would no longer be frustrating. That had been my assumed solution.

My inner being responded with a question back to me.

"Why on earth would you make yourself choose a food on the buffet that you don't like when you have other choices? Give yourself permission to choose the one you do like . . . that you love, because the only way that you would want to 'alter' yourself is if it's a better you."

Fuck. That made so much sense. I was not to accommodate anyone on the planet that may or may not be in alignment.

I had been fixated on the different Abraham discussions where the person on stage would ask about leaving their partner or having an issue, and then Abraham would suggest they make a list of positive aspects about their partner. The result would be that their vortex relationship would manifest. They wouldn't need to go anywhere for it.

But my inner being pointed out that Abraham had also said sometimes the answer is to leave. Both are options.

Then they asked me, "How does it feel to leave . . . first impulses."

I responded that it felt scary. They asked me what I was scared of. I could immediately sense that it was my fear of hurting him that terrified me.

More questions came.

"Is that alignment?"

"What do you think the solution is?"

"Do you want Reid, or do you want him?"

Those were easy enough to answer. I wanted Reid. I wanted ease.

"Do you have ease?"

"Do you agree that you want more than you have now?"

"Does your energy feel light and free?"

These questions were so illuminating. They quickly got to the root of how I was truly feeling because the old belief systems were not included in this series of questions.

My intention to live a life of abundance, clarity, and ease and to live it all at a fast pace had been calling forward this information and this moment of clarity. My nonphysical self was giving me what I was calling for, what I was desiring.

I had assumed that I needed to simply work on myself and change myself to resolve the frustration I felt in my relationship. I had been rearranging my own Rubik's Cube to the pace that he wanted to live his life.

"Do I like who I am when I'm in this relationship?"

"Is this truly what I want, yes or no?"

"Does this work for me, yes or no?"

The great work for me to do is get to the place where I can own the yes or no.

Source Energy is *never* going to ask me to stay in a situation that is uncomfortable or cumbersome, that requires me to have to change so much about myself for it to "work."

Am I doing him a service or disservice by staying with someone that I have to work this hard to love?

As I considered these questions, I definitely felt love for him. But what I began to realize was that I needed to accept that it was ok to outgrow someone.

It's okay. Anything is okay. I had been so frozen on this idea that if I was truly aligned, then he could be fully himself and it wouldn't have to frustrate me.

But the eureka moment that was coming into focus for me was that it also wouldn't mean I had to want to be in a relationship with him.

He's on this note over here on the piano and I'm on this note. I can let that be okay.

And I can love and admire him from afar and be appreciative for all that contrast has put into my vortex. And now I'm clearer in what I want in a relationship with a man.

My inner being pointed out that I could literally do every single thing my partner thought he wanted me to do, and he still wouldn't be happy. Because happiness only comes from inside. Confidence, groundedness, certainty . . . that's an inside job all the time. I could spend the rest of my life pouring into him to make sure he's "okay."

I honestly was trying to work on myself so that he could be however he needed to be or was just naturally . . . and it didn't need to frustrate me. Or piss me off.

All feelings are ok, all emotions are okay. But how much spiritual work did I need to do so he could just be a-okay, and do we even need to do spiritual work? Or could I say, "I've got the clarity now that I don't like that. That is guidance from my nonphysical self. So what do I want to do about it? What do I do next?"

I knew that the answer could be either "Let's work on this together" or "Let's separate." Those were the two options, and it didn't resonate to work on it. I didn't want to prolong something that I could feel I no longer wanted.

How did it feel to realize I wanted freedom . . . how did that freedom feel? I had the thought, "Wow I listened to my inner being and I'm trusting that's true." This relationship with my partner was an amazing season and I loved it, and I appreciated it, and I was going to give myself permission to BE and DO this point of attraction. Today it just didn't work for me anymore. It had worked for me but then it didn't. I was going to give myself permission that that was okay. I matter and my preferences matter a lot. AND I was going to trust that he is Source Energy in a physical body. And we attract experiences. This was not insurmountable.

I had been so focused on not wanting to hurt my partner that I hadn't focused on what I truly wanted for me. I wanted to see him as pure love, pure light on a journey, growing and expanding. I realized he could be much happier with someone who adores him as he is. Someone who adores the parts that piss me off because there is someone out there like that.

It's hard to be light about it because it has historically stressed me out like nothing else. But I knew there's nothing serious going on. We are eternal beings.

Which one was better? I actually wanted freedom. I wanted fun. I wanted joy and I did want to follow my impulses. So, I was going to trust that I'm going to get better and better, braver and braver. And eventually I'll see there was no need for bravery. Nothing serious going on right here. And it's my nonphysical me leading the way.

Calling Clarity and Freedom to My Path

As the session with KT continued, my inner being explained that if I don't trust myself, life doesn't work. The only way for me to keep perfection is through change.

They continued by telling me that the best thing I could do for anyone was to see them as pure love and light. See them that way, and let their journey be however it unfolds. I had been buying into the lie that his happiness was dependent upon me. I understood on a cognitive level that it wasn't but my terror of breaking up with him was still rooted deeply in that perspective.

I didn't want a life of struggling. I wanted a life of ease. I was going to give myself permission to want what I wanted. And to let go of whatever it was in my life that didn't work.

"You're getting softer. Do you feel it?" they asked.

"Yeah. That all made sense," I said softly.

"Of course it does . . . we're collective consciousness! Got ya again . . . hahaha. And we told KT that this would be an hour-long session, by the way?"

Even before my session began wrapping up, I knew what I was ready to do. As uncomfortable as I felt, I intended to break up with him that night. But I wanted it to somehow feel like ease. I wanted to feel good. I wanted to always feel good.

That's where the power is. I want to feel good, or at least feel steady, even when it feels like upheaval. And I understood that I couldn't calibrate to however he chose to react. I just wanted to feel *my* source. And I wanted to take a moment to appreciate that the only reason this stressed me out was because I do care so deeply. And it wasn't a decision I'd taken lightly.

"And since you are in tune with your intention to be kind and to stay connected to Source, the path for it to unfold already exists," offered my inner being.

It felt really good to know that. So, as I navigated the break-up discussion, I simply planned to follow inspired impulses for what to say and when.

My inner being reminded me of an experience I had a month or two earlier when two of my dearest friends announced that they had gone from friends to a romantic couple. The feelings I felt when I heard that news (all that clarity and intense emotion of love blowing my socks off with an example of how exceptional and crazy fun a relationship could be) was my nonphysical self, pouring into every pore of my body the feeling of my vortex. It was *not* just great information to have and then do nothing. I had a really powerful emotional response to it and I went from joy and elation to looking at my current relationship and my vibration went way down.

I asked myself, "Which felt better? My response of awe and amazement when I looked at my friends' relationship or my own relationship?"

Of course, my friends' relationship was lightyears beyond what I felt about my own relationship.

I want to have that relationship. Then it was just a simple realization of wow, what I have now, is it what I want? And the honest answer from me was no. I realized that I had been getting hung up because I was judging myself for the "no" *and* I was so focused on my partner's feelings, which I could never control. That's why my nonphysical self gave the example that I could be every single thing he claimed he wanted, and he would still lash out at me in anger.

His nonphysical self will take care of him . . . easily! It knows every path for him easily.

I realized that by being scared to hurt him I had been calibrating to another person. I didn't want to feel that way.

What I wanted to let go of is how I had also felt in my breakup with my wife. I had been terrified to hurt her and stayed in a situation that wasn't right for either of us.

My inner being asked me if I wanted to keep repeating that pattern even if I broke up with my partner. I would have the exact same pattern until I did the inner work of knowing it's absolutely okay to want what I want, to know it immediately, and then make changes instantly in my life. What I want matters.

I could have said no, this is what I want. I don't care where you're at in your vibration or your energy or your job or what you're doing. This is what I want. And it's okay to want what I want.

And then that was it. I would no longer stay in a situation that didn't fit what I wanted or what I preferred.

I realized that I needed to be more tuned in to what I wanted and not so accommodating to others.

It's okay to want more.

And since I didn't feel chill or lighthearted about this, that just told me that I needed to align with how my nonphysical self felt about it. Ask myself, "What is my truth?" then hear it and feel it. And then examine what it is inside me that's not letting me move forward in my truth.

As the session wound to a close, they told me, "Know that we love you. And that you're pure love and, really, we promise, nothing serious is going on here. You've already known this, but you weren't ready for this at the beginning of your coaching sessions. But you knew it and we've just been waiting for you to bring it up. All is well. There's great love here for you. Now talk to KT. She's very wise. Even when we're not flowing through her. Namaste."

The Breakup

From my session with KT, I went straight to dinner. My partner and I already had plans to follow dinner with Abby who was going to give us readings from her tarot cards. The cards delivered powerful messages to him and me, so when everyone left, I knew this was the time to have the dreaded conversation.

"Let's sit down and talk." As we sat on the couch, I ripped off the band aid and said that I no longer wanted to be in the relationship. He rejected the idea outright.

He said, "I refuse to throw away our relationship without a fight."

The words came to me: "this isn't a negotiation." I was very clear on my path, and it wasn't to work with a counselor. It was to follow where my nonphysical self was calling me, and I trusted it. And the clarity was to no longer be in a relationship with him.

The great thing about clarity is that there's no mistaking it. There's no uncertainty. I've come to realize now that because I have been experiencing more and more clarity on many subjects, that I have come to prize clarity over all else. Even when it is a surprise. Even when it scares the shit out of me. My only choice is to walk in the direction I'm calling myself. I trust myself more than my need to make others happy or comfortable. Although this conversation was something I dreaded most, I knew the discomfort wouldn't last forever. I had so many breakthrough realizations during the seminar that day that I felt the truth of those ideas gave me a powerful resolve to navigate that conversation with confidence. And although my partner felt the need to revisit the conversation many more times over the days and weeks that followed, the freedom I desired had been initiated. It took four full months for him to move out, but I persevered each day to calibrate to my sense of peace and joy and alignment.

This reminded me of when I hit a wall while trying to navigate my identity as a gay man. I had run out of any other perspective or support from my family and church and everything I had been taught to that point. I still remember vividly that point of realizing it was now down to me and me alone. Since no one was going to say it's ok to be gay, I remember thinking, "What if everyone else is wrong?"

I distinctly decided that I had to choose myself and trust that I was right. Now I have such clarity and practiced independence that I can easily feel into, "What feels true for me?" And then ask, "What is presenting itself as a reason to not act on my truth?" That's resistance. That's calibrating to someone else's truth. The clearer I get, the simpler it feels to check in with myself when I'm feeling an internal tug of war.

Shedding My Old Life: Getting Paid to Do Nothing

As I navigated living under the same roof with the person I'd just broken up with, I decided to travel to allow myself some space alone to process this new breakup. We lived in my loft, which is open by design and tight quarters to inhabit while he figured out where he would relocate. I decided to finally go to Rome for ten days. That felt like a wonderful place to reflect and heal.

While in Rome, I received an email from my corporate HR department. I was being offered a full year's salary plus three additional bonuses if I chose to retire early. Hmmm.

My job had always been a security blanket for me (as it is for most humans). Health benefits and a regular paycheck equaled security. But I had been calling forth more freedom to my path, less obligations and more fun.

My first reaction was a no. I had assumed I would have a new opportunity to make money or receive a surprise pile of money so that I could simply quit my job. But here it was. An opportunity to have a steady paycheck and travel with no schedule other than my own curiosity leading the way.

The more I relaxed into the idea and felt my way through it, I could feel that I was ready to trust the universe in a new way. I knew that my inner being had my back and all of nonphysical's support, which included the resources of the universe raining down all around me. Always.

Soon that initial nauseous feeling gave way to eager anticipation. Afterward, every time I felt scared, I returned to a recorded session with KT where we had discussed this new opportunity to be free.

I started the session by sharing an awareness I felt on my last day in Rome. I considered booking a tour of the Borghese Villa. In addition, I had planned to book a restaurant that had been highly recommended as well. But I specifically felt the soft guidance, "No, I want to have no obligations and no reservations." I wanted the freedom to respond to whatever crossed my path. And sure enough, I met a new friend. She was in line at the pharmacy where I was getting my negative Covid test documentation that allowed me to fly back to the United States. It was such a great example of the law of attraction where we were a vibrational match. We hit it off instantly. We spent the day together and it just kept unfolding spontaneously. I could see that I was listening to my impulses to stay open for whatever might cross my path and sure enough, fun experiences were showing up on my path.

My inner being asked me if I thought I'd live life more that way, just chasing the wind?

When I responded with a yes, they agreed with, "We think so too."

Then they asked me what I wanted to do next.

I explained that throughout my day I often asked myself, "What's next? What's fun? What do I want to do next? What's ready?"

My team of nonphysical observed that my energy of switching to just a pure "well what's fun and what's next?" was the result of having shifted my belief system to the truth of who I am and that there's nothing missing. I wasn't missing anything. I was no longer seeking or going to any experience so that I'd feel better or so I could know I was worthy. All of that was completely gone. They encouraged me to really sit in that.

They asked me again: "What's next?"

As I scanned my mind for what I felt like might be "next," they highlighted that they had asked me twice. "First impulse," they continued.

They must have known that I was thinking about my opportunity to retire early and receive a year's worth of pay as incentive to voluntarily leave.

My inner being reminded me that I had been calling in expected and unexpected money and that a bonus for retiring had never crossed my mind.

This was the perfect example that as you continue to enjoy just living life (and fall deeper and deeper into a trust) it's normal to think about something and know you're going to get it. There's no having to figure it out. Nothing is ever complicated. When you're in free-flowing energy, there is nothing that's ever complicated. It's just happily skipping along one step to the next, to the next, to the next. This is how a unicorn lives! All I was focused on was loving the idea of expected and unexpected money coming my way. And that's what the universe could deliver.

I never had to think about *how* that would happen. Because if I had done that, I would have gone into more questioning energy instead of free-flowing energy. And it would literally slow the very thing that I wanted. And I would have slowed on an even deeper level; I would have slowed myself down from living at the speed I came to live. It wasn't necessarily that I was slowing my vortex down or pinching it off. It was actually just me slowing myself down, pinching myself off from everything that's available to me.

So back to that realization that I had just asked for expected and unexpected money. I asked for fun new ways money could come into my life, or for large sums of money. And then there it was, a path literally right in front of me and I didn't even ask for it. I didn't ask for "and I want to retire." I'd always talked about just simply going on to new projects or different things that are more fun.

The early retirement package felt like a logical next step . . . plus I knew that I could say yes to "considering" the package and would still be allowed to back out of it closer to the final decision deadline. This felt good. It felt like ease.

"So, are you going to retire, yes or no? First impulse . . . you already had it . . ." This yes or no question format was very clarifying! It quickly cut through indecisiveness to uncover the feeling place of my truth.

My answer was definitely a yes but only because I had already taken several days of stopping to meditate and feel my energy on this topic. I was being shown that hesitating to answer actually affected my momentum. By checking in with myself and feeling my emotions, it showed me that I was in a new place of trusting the universe to provide for me. Trusting Me to provide for me. The old me looked at my job as my safety net. And although I experienced a brief panic at the thought of letting the job go, as I felt further into it, I realized I had released that old belief and was in a new understanding of how the universe works. And since I'd acknowledged this new confidence, I was able to move into the new phase of the excitement that I really could just go wherever and explore. How much time did I want to spend here or there? I could enjoy following my impulses—simply enjoy life and enjoy the fun and enjoy the fact that I know that with every single desire I have, the bigger part of me knows it and is going to deliver it. Is *already* delivering it. And I get to continue to line up with that truth. Life really is meant to be easy; it really is meant to be fun. I could give myself complete permission to be in a super yummy phase of, "Yes, I want the desires I put out there. I want them to flow in, and I love them flowing in and I freely accept them flowing in."

I could be at a place where I'd live in such freedom that I didn't need the plan anymore. Before, my logical mind would need all one hundred steps. And then I would go over the steps again, to make certain I didn't miss anything. And now I was in a place of not needing to know the steps. I knew it all works out. I was just in tune with "What do I really want?" Because anything is possible. I could go to Australia, I could go to New Zealand, I could go to Mexico, I could go to Ecuador. I could go to the Arctic Circle if I wanted to.

"You get that kind of freedom, Reid. And you've given it to yourself. You have kind of built up your own empowerment and truth. Because you've let it in. And you followed the impulses way back when. Whether it was listening to Abraham, or reading a book, or going to a seminar, or searching for this or that, or trusting the impulse to 'oh, I want to do that. I want to have a session with KT.' And we really want to point out that it was *you* that did it, because when you had your first session with KT, you didn't know her at all. You just trusted the impulse that it sounded like fun. 'I want to do that.' And it's always been you listening to your guidance system. And now you can see and you have that knowing in your body that this really is true."

Wow. It felt good to let that soak in. It's *me* doing it. What am I ready for next? What do I want to do next?

I've also shifted to an awareness of, "Wow, I can get ready for something really, really fast. And now I trust that if I'm thinking about it, I need to pay attention to that." It's not just a random thought, or just a pipe dream, or just a "Oh, well, that'll be off in the future sometime." I've learned to bring it into the now. Let it be now. And then the next step and the next step. And it's quite an exciting journey. Imagine how even better it will continue to be as the momentum builds.

What I Want Presents Itself

It was time for another session with KT. I was excited to further discuss my early retirement opportunity because I had worked past the initial split energy of leaving my security-blanket job that I had been in for twenty-three years.

I was excited about what it really meant, all that freedom!

As I explained where I was emotionally, my higher self wanted to discuss it further. What happened that enabled me to release the split energy and allow the feeling of clear, enthusiastic energy?

When the offer first presented itself, my original thought process was simply thinking, "Well, I have this wonderful job and the path of least resistance would be just to have something new present itself, either a fortune or a higher paying job that excites me and allows travel." And then I would just quit my job and sail off into the sunset. So to quit my job even with some months of salary that's paid and not have anything lined up was, at first, an obvious new place for me. So, it took me some time to expand or relax into that.

But it was identical to other areas of my life where something was changing or something new was unfolding. I felt the discomfort, but then I lined up with it. And then I could feel my way through it and into it. I could feel myself find that place inside me that I had already expanded to but needed to actually catch up to it. So that all of me had the clarity.

Said another way, I had that first initial feeling of panic of "whoa, whoa, wait a minute." And I was able to start to breathe through it and say, "Well . . . maybe?"

It wasn't (1) feel panic, and then (2) immediately jump to peace and "Oh, it's perfect. Whatever I decide is perfect." But it was beautiful. It was, "Well, maybe it would be okay. And let me think about this tomorrow. And what would that possibility be? And what would this possibility be? And okay, well, maybe I did call this in. And maybe I didn't. I don't know, let me look through it." And it was that same exact process that helps me in every single area of my life, every single area of anything I'm dreaming of. And that process is actually part of what I've been after. To get clear on my truth and the fact that I am nonphysical energy.

"So, what did you decide?" asked my inner being.

I explained that I had been meditating by re-listening to the previous session from a few days before. Every time I would listen to our discussion, I felt like I was really into the "oh my god, this is so exciting" energy. This was exactly everything I'd been calling to my path, and this made sense. This was how I wanted to live. I wanted to trust the universe to give me what I need as I needed it.

At this point in our session, my inner being wanted to add and fine tune my thought process by clarifying an important but nuanced distinction: It is beneficial for me to have the same excitement about either decision, whether to take the retirement or whether to say, "Thanks for the offer but no, I'm good." And to understand that there's equal excitement that can be felt on either one of those paths because either is perfect. It was simply up to me what kind of journey I wanted to experience.

I would have never thought about it that way. I could see how life changing these sessions were. Although one could make the case that I had absolutely been the one to call this information forward by choosing to work with KT, who was my path of least resistance or as Abraham would say, my path of most allowance. MOST ALLOWANCE for sure!

When I was asked in the previous session, do I want to retire early or not . . . just tell me your first impulse. The answer was, "Well, of course, yes." Since I didn't have to worry about the "how," if I was really being consistent with what I wanted and how I wanted to live, then it would be a "hell yes!" And I was excited for the new opportunities and the newer freedom. This was everything I'd been asking for.

Whatever I want, whatever I ask for, the answer is yes. And when I tune in to that energy and keep following the impulses in that direction, absolutely what I want presents itself. What I desire starts unfolding.

Sometimes the unfolding is very easily recognizable. And sometimes it's more of a, "I don't know what this is, but I know how it feels. And it definitely feels like a yes and it definitely feels like the next logical step. And the bigger part of me knows that I like details and knows I like plans."

I now live in my knowing that this is how it works. This is exciting!

The Power of Saying Yes to Ourselves

The important key to absolutely every new horizon, every desire being manifested is right there! It's me trusting me . . . that I know the next logical step. That everything really is taken care of. I can never get too far out ahead in figuring out the "how" since that's never my job. It's understanding and living the process of: the ONLY way to get to the step AFTER the one in front of me is to take the step that is right in front of me. Period. One step at a time, just as we've always heard and been taught.

Zooming out on my life revealed a filter I'd never recognized before. I realized that our biggest milestones boil down to the times when we have said yes to ourselves. Walking away from my relationship and the comfort of my corporate job were two significant examples of me saying yes to myself. Leaving my marriage and coming out as gay was a *massive* yes to myself.

Abundance

I am abundance. I've always been abundant. All my body's systems are being ordered and operated by Source Energy on my behalf. That's abundance. My heart has beaten billions of times on my behalf so that

I don't have to think about it. I don't have to remember how or when to breathe. When I sleep, my lungs breathe and my heart beats without me doing anything. That *is* abundance. I've been abundant all along.

Similarly, money and resources flow to me without me needing to do anything. Opportunities, resources, experiences, and people are even being coordinated on my behalf while I sleep.

As I understand in a deeper way than ever that I *am* abundance, that's all I can find. I can now reside in the magnitude of the now, noticing, celebrating, and relishing every variation and form of abundance and fun crossing my path, flowing right to me. I have that feeling of "*now* is my time!"

I often think of how perfectly a specific piece of music captures this feeling that the world is lined up to deliver to me and knock my socks off. That all eyes are focused on me, interested in what can be done for me and standing by, ready to delight me. I think of the climactic scene from *Hello Dolly* (of course I do) where Dolly is at the top of the grand staircase of the prestigious Harmonia Gardens. After an absence from social circles following the passing of her husband, Dolly is reemerging back into society and tonight is the big unveiling. The entire staff has lovingly awaited her return to a place she had frequented so often. They are excited to receive her. There is a frenzied energy in the air as they make everything perfect for her arrival. Suddenly the room goes silent as they realize she has arrived. As the frantic discussions between the waiters and maître d' screech to a stop, the camera pans up to find Dolly Levi in all her glory at the top of the gilded staircase. And now the music kicks into this perfect melodic embodiment of "I came to slay and the world is my mother fuckin' oyster."

Confident, regal, poised, fully embodied in her own power, she stands and takes in the moment. Barbra embodies this through every cell of her body. The music kicks in and she slyly, slowly descends the staircase appreciating all that are focused on her and appreciating them too. So, with all that meaning baked into this cinematic moment, I now picture Dolly in her big, elaborate Saturday night hat and golden dress boarding the cruise ship or going to the grocery store. OMG that's vibrationally *me*. Smiling from ear to ear at the humor of it all, I feel the energy and ease and magic of understanding this is how the universe feels about me. Everywhere I go, I'm in *that* triumphant energy. That is how the universe sees me and yields to me. Happily, extravagantly, automatically. Oooooh . . . the magnitude of NOW.

Big ME Loving Little Me

I had a cool breakthrough in November of 2022. This was technically three months beyond the official twelve months of my experiment. This exciting realization was that everything that was showing up for me in my life that felt good was the same theme of Me loving me, my inner being me loving physical me. Said another way, spiritual me loving human me. I was now on my sixth Abraham Hicks cruise which sailed from Sydney Australia to New Zealand. I found myself in an onboard romance that was a vortex-level experience. And I could tell that the love I felt coming from this person was really coming from my inner being and therefore I wasn't dependent on this person to love me. It was actually me loving me, and this person was a vibrational match to my love for myself and to my vortex, so as a result, we matched up.

And I realized that when I'm looking for my next home, and I find something that blows my mind and thrills me, that's also my inner being loving me. It's Me loving me. Everything in the universe is available to my inner being, so there are infinite ways for me to feel and create because it's always Me loving me. It's never outside of me; it's never exterior. It's always Me loving me. There are so many endless ways for that to show up. It makes creation way more logical, and it makes creation feel like it's not big or small. It's just all the millions of ways that I love me because I am the universe and already include all that exists. So of course, I can create and summon absolutely anything and everything. It's Me loving me.

I am the universe.

I love knowing the dimensions of me, the two measures of me. It really feels amazing when I'm walking down the street to understand myself in a bigger way. Seeing myself and the world around me while knowing that not only do I get to tune to the magic but at the same exact time that I *am* the magic.

In the same exact moment, I am the kid set loose in the candy store and I *am* the candy store.

I'm not only living from a place of knowing but I *am* the knowing. I *am* all that is known.

I *am* the universe. I include it all.

Every wave on the beach whispers to me, "You are loved, you are loved, you are loved" and at the same moment . . . I *am* Love.

I am both tuning *to* a portal of frequency and infinite intelligence and . . . . I *am* the portal.

I *am* what I seek.

I *am* a creator, and I *am* the creation.

Note

1. Marilyn Monroe, *Quotespedia*, accessed Oct. 2023, https://www.quotespedia.org/authors /m/marilyn-monroe/everything-happens-for-a-reason-people-change-so-you-can-learn-to -let-go-things-go-wrong-so-you-can-appreciate-them-when-theyre-right-marilyn-monroe/.

Chapter 8

THE UNICORN TRAIL

Discovering and Isolating the YES Energy in Barcelona

ONE OF THE BIGGEST THINGS I'VE LEARNED, WHICH HAS transformed how I now navigate my life as a unicorn, happened while on vacation in Barcelona at the end of May.

I was now traveling as a single person, but I felt stressed out about being "out in the fray" again. Part of me wanted to say I'm never taking my clothes off in front of another human being again. It had been six years of feeling comfortable with my partner, but not comfortable with my body. And soon I would have to take my clothes off in front of brand-new people? So even though I had downloaded the Grindr and Scruff apps so that I could see from a safe distance the current community of men, I was not ready emotionally to dive in or ramp up my energy for something as stressful as being intimate with a new person.

I put in my profile that I was *not* looking to hook up. Many people are there to just chat and window shop (of course there are those who are there to find a lover too).

One guy had been messaging me over the last several days. From the way he conducted himself and the way he had written his profile, I could tell he was an intelligent, more emotionally evolved man. And I noticed he was intimidatingly attractive.

He was only thirty-six and he was extremely fit, whereas I was a little fit but closer to just normal. But he was very interested and kept reaching out and making conversation. At one point he asked if I would like to meet him for a drink. I told him that I was not looking to hook up but that if he was still interested in meeting to chat over a drink, I would be up for that. I had been eating meals by myself and walking around and enjoying my own company. But the thought of socializing with another person without the expectation of being intimate sounded wonderful.

What was important and life-changing at this point in the decision process was I could sense an energy strand of "yes." Once I had removed the stress of sex out of the equation, I could feel pure yes energy. It most likely came in the form of feeling and thinking "that would be fun . . . I want to do this." So, I agreed with that qualifier and he responded that he had read my profile and understood that I was not "looking." He was cool with that. What a gentleman! The reason this was significant was I felt I was guided to notice that moment where I could feel the specific yes energy and then from there make my decision.

The First Step

An important element was making a decision only one step out in front of me (meeting him for a cocktail). Full stop. If I had tried to make that same decision two or three steps out from the cocktail meeting, I would've felt stressed out and I would have said no. I arrived at the time and place (at a gay bar) and found a seat at a table inside and waited for him to arrive. I had not spent the whole day worried about anything. When he arrived, he sat down next to me and was smiling from ear to ear. He was delighted with me. His eyes were so full of joy, happiness, and satisfaction. I could feel the energy exchange between us.

We ordered a drink and started chatting about our careers and our travels. After a short time, he stopped and said, "Your smile is so amazing" and "You are so handsome!" It wasn't just his words. Everything about his energy communicated to my energetic core that I was safe, I was appreciated, I was attractive to him, and as a result, I felt emotionally safe to relax and be present in that moment. I was more than just comfortable; I was matching his energy of enthusiasm. The result was surprising. I couldn't keep my hands off him. I rested one of my hands lightly on his knee as I faced him in my chair. After several minutes of getting to know each other and both of us smiling from ear to ear, I asked him if I could kiss him!

What I found fascinating about all of this is I went from being shut off and feeling insecure to feeling confident and downright bold in this situation because the energy was next level. The attraction was palpable. And since we are energetic beings, it was *felt* with no effort. I remember realizing a week before that as much as I wanted to experience ease in travel, I wanted to also feel ease in not only relationships but also in sexual hookups that were only designed to last an evening. I wanted to feel ease in everything I did and in everything I experienced.

The Kiss

And here it was, the most amazing ease I've ever felt on a first date or hookup. Never mind a first date experience following a six-year relationship. As we kissed it felt amazing, the energy and the rhythm was so delicious and sexy. We talked some more and then we kissed some more. And then I heard myself ask him, "Would you like to come back to my hotel?" He did not hesitate and said yes and off we went holding hands and appreciating the exchange of attraction between the two of us. I kept thinking, "I can't believe what is about to happen!" I thought I wasn't ready and now suddenly here I am ready to take this sweet sexy man back to my hotel room for sex.

This was a powerful example for me to see that when I made one decision based on the yes energy, I could trust not knowing what step two and step three were going to be. I could just trust and proceed with step one. What's cool about the experience was he was beautiful, he was ridiculously fit, he was almost twenty years younger than me, and he was delighted with me. As he took off his clothes and it became clear exactly how fit he was, I thought for a second, "Easy for you to be eager to take your clothes off and get naked when you look like that!" And now it was my turn. As I stripped down to my underwear, he was taking me in and said enthusiastically, "You're beautiful" AND he was being sincere! I could feel that he wasn't just saying it by the look on his face and the way he said it. Plus, his body was exhibiting that he was in fact, aroused by me. So now I could just relax and be fully present in our mutual appreciation of each other.

What a wonderful baptism into my new life as a single man. I learned from that experience that I could trust my ability to make decisions when they were coming from a place of yes energy. I learned when I was in that space of preferring to feel real chemistry, I could feel comfortable and confident—and *that* was going to be my new normal. I decided from that point on I would not jump into bed with someone unless I felt real chemistry and real mutual appreciation. Feeling a connection and a palpable exchange of energy was way too satisfying to go without. I could acknowledge someone was physically appealing but still not feel actual desire for them. Now I would insist on feeling desire for the person, not just the desire for the act we both were looking for.

Here We Go Again

So that was an important touchstone for me. A week later and near the end of my trip to Spain, I was meditating and felt the same yes energy to accept an invitation to fly to Manchester, UK, and meet a guy who had been messaging me for about three weeks. I had rejected these invitations for the last three weeks because I felt it was too extravagant to change my airfare and travel to another country for such a small thing as a first date. I had just left a relationship and I didn't feel the need to change my itinerary and fly from Spain to the UK to meet anyone. So that had been my mental state for the last three weeks. But suddenly during meditation, I got this impulse to say yes. And since I had recognized that yes energy and knew I was safe to follow it, I expected that good things would come from it.

I started changing all of my travel plans to return to the US from Spain and make a new detour and stop through Manchester for a few days. Instead of it feeling overwhelming or tedious to book new flights and cancel my previous flights in addition to finding a hotel in Manchester, I looked at it as just one step in front of the other to follow through on inspired action.

What surprised me was that once I arrived around 8:00 p.m., he didn't drive over to meet me at my hotel for a drink. The night was young, people! Especially for someone who had flown from Spain just to meet him. He figured he would see me for dinner after work the next day. Ok. That didn't have to be a problem even though I'd gone through extraordinary effort and inconvenience to accommodate his desire to meet me before I returned to the US. I was feeling steady no matter what. Yes, I was aware that he wasn't meeting me halfway but my desire to feel good unconditionally was stronger.

The next day we had dinner, and we did some light sightseeing but there was simply no chemistry. After he dropped me off at my hotel, he didn't ask to come up. I remember feeling puzzled and wondering to the universe, "Why did I come to Manchester?" We had exchanged only one grandma kiss. It's what we call a peck on the lips. He texted me later, "I can't wait to hold you and kiss you." I almost laughed out loud. Really?! You could have fooled me!

The Morning After

The next morning, as I walked down the sidewalk, I was lightly pondering, "Why did I feel such a specific yes energy to make such an elaborate and expensive detour?" And the words came to me: "I didn't come here for a client or to meet someone that would offer me a job. I didn't come here for a relationship. I came here to witness how much I've grown and how dramatically I've changed. You came here *for you*. I am the manifestation."

I had been feeling for months that something *big* was going to happen on this trip to Spain. Something was going to change my life, and I had just assumed it was going to be me meeting a new client, getting a new job offer, maybe meeting a man who would surprise me, and I would realize, "Oh this is why I am single and free . . . to be ready to meet this handsome Arabian prince who is going to change my life!"

However, the old me would have never been so spontaneous and ready to follow energy to a different country. But now I was so trusting and ready and flexible and tuned to my yes energy that I had come here so I could stand from my new perspective and understand and realize *what* I had become and *who* I had become. And to just make sure I didn't miss the significance of the words I was receiving, a wave of emotion swept in to punctuate the realization. As if to say, "This is a big deal! You are the creation. *You* are the finale!"

The Big Reveal

I knew the trip was going to be big and those were the only things I could think of that felt as big as what I expected would happen. I loved the surprise twist in the plot that it wasn't about anyone or anything outside of me. It was me! I was the crescendo of the trip. I was the manifestation. It was about me recognizing how far I'd come.

This almost brought me to tears. I noticed a new, recurring phenomenon, which was to receive a concept or an understanding or an awareness of something and it would be followed with a wave of emotion. It seemed like an emotional punctuation making sure I didn't miss it. I love this new punctuation because it shows me that I am caught up with my most expanded version of myself, of who I have become. Months later I received clarification that what I felt wasn't Source Energy sending an emotional punctuation through me. It was the human me feeling myself intertwined with the Source Energy me. The emotion I felt was actually a manifestation of this aligned, intertwined state I was in.

Either way it definitely choked me up because I could feel in my bones and in every cell of my body the magnitude of my transformation. And our own transformation, our becoming the fullest versions of ourselves is what our eternal journey has always been about!

Chapter 9

A UNICORN ENDING

What's the Meaning of Life? Why Are We Here?

DID WE COME TO BE RICH OR TRAVEL OR HEAL A SICK PLANET? Did we come to fix other people? Did we come to be perfect and religious? No. We certainly didn't come to accomplish a long list of chores.

In one of my sessions, I was fascinated when my conversation with my inner being revealed exactly this. My nonphysical self came right out and explained to physically focused me why we wanted to become physical and return to this earthly plane. We came to the earthly realm to have expanding experiences. We came for the joy of becoming more and having fun and playing. When we were nonphysical, we were all so eager to play when we returned to Earth. That was our number one focus: "Let's go play again. Because it's so fun."

We were so clear: nothing important was happening here. Everything was already in perfect balance and just getting better and better and better. And that's why well-being is always intact. And you're simply here playing; you're expanding, having experiences. And the earth is so beautifully balanced that when you do things like kill a lot of trees or kill a lot of fish, nonphysical has got it covered. It's okay. It's a process. Life continues to evolve. We haven't lost anything.

Humans get focused on the extinction of animals and while that may be true, there are more species, more life coming.

There are all kinds of new things to discover . . . more, more, more. And as more people live the way they intended to live when they came, the more radical changes you will see on the planet: more discoveries, more fun, better ways to do things, and it always balances out. It gets even better and better. The same is true for your life. Because you've become even more of what you intended to live. And now you're in a position of receiving; you are in receptive mode, and you're letting all of that free flow pour back in.

In one of my KT sessions, we discussed that I was on the brink of a new shift of more understanding, bigger awareness, more clarity, more eternal knowing.

My inner being pointed out that it continues to happen daily in my journey. That each meditation is that much clearer. Each moment that I pick up on the impulse of Source Energy . . . of the true me admiring something through my eyes or enjoying anything with my senses. Those things are really me as Source Energy, enjoying and being what I intended to be. I was encouraged to really think about that as I walked outside and saw beautiful flowers or trees. And to think about it when I saw something that took my breath away, like a stunning building that inspires awe and admiration.

When I have that pure moment, that's me as nonphysical energy. Living exactly the moment I intended to . . . the *way* I intended to feel it in that moment. It's me coming into physical form to *enjoy* being in physical form, to enjoy all that's here. To enjoy the rain, the smell of grass, the feel of the wind on my skin. I came to truly enjoy the planet. Enjoy the *fun* of this atmosphere, this playground, this perfectly balanced ecosystem, this extraordinary, absolutely extraordinary universe that is in perfect flow and perfect blend. Because when I was in nonphysical, I was so clear and aware of how much really was happening vibrationally in a moment, and how beautifully in sync the entire thing was. My inner being wanted to stress that those moments that almost take my breath away or that cause tingles all over my body, I'm in tune. That is me in "nonphysical," truly enjoying my physical body.

And truly enjoying all of creation. My inner being continued to stress that this is something deep to remember and know: "This is me in my true form, enjoying my body, enjoying creation." To remember to really take a moment and grasp that and remember something in my life that completely took my breath away. And know that was me in the purest form of alignment with my nonphysical cells. The real me, the true me, the energy that creates worlds.

Wow . . . I loved receiving that from my session! That was life changing.

There's something really satisfying and comforting about the key to life being pure and simple.

That's what appealed to me about my year-long focus on "fun" as a scientific thought experiment. That simplicity compelled me to write this book. The simplicity of focusing my mind on having, feeling, and "being" fun. And knowing in my bones that the result would be a transformed life. A unicorn life of never-ending magic. Everything I desire will flow to me while all of life's little transactional, logistical details will take care of themselves in this process of truly *living* fun.

I was on the phone with one of my new friends, Candice, and she used my first Alaska cruise and my recent second Alaska cruise as striking book ends framing up how much my life had truly changed in the space of twelve months. For some reason, thinking of my year in this new way of everything happening between two Alaska cruises felt even more dramatic.

Just as I had expected, my life is unrecognizable. I am free on so many levels. Free to move through life faster than I ever thought I could. Now I'm no longer in the structure of anything. Not the structure of a corporate job or a romantic relationship that doesn't fulfill me.

I was having breakfast by myself at my favorite restaurant in St. Louis and it dawned on me that I wanted to add a bit more detail to the "before and after" of my life following the completion of my first twelve months of this experiment. Here are those highlights I shared at the opening of my book plus a few more details:

- I'm on fire with joy. No matter what I'm doing or where I'm going, I feel an exhilaration inside my body. This has always been the goal. To feel unconditional joy and love for life and myself. I sincerely wish this feeling for everyone. How many people can say they feel on fire with joy? This alone is enough. This is how a unicorn feels!

- I'm choosing to work on creative projects that thrill me even if there isn't a practical end result that I'm aware of. Simply following the call of what thrills me.

- I'm no longer working. Full stop. That is a radical change. Instead of turning in timesheets, I now wake up when I want, do what I want when I want.

- I'm now an entrepreneur who tunes to the unicorn frequency when deciding what to invest in. Before I was terrified of leaving my corporate security blanket and now, I'm letting the universe yield to me as I need it. That's a radical "personality" change. That's shifting the source of my security from conditions outside of me back to where the source of my security belongs . . . me. I'm the abundance!

- I'm single. I had no plans to leave my relationship and then I realized my today preferences are new and different than they were six years ago or even six months ago. My willingness to acknowledge the clarity of my preferences and following my own calling to feel better by leaving the relationship has transformed my now reality. I realize I love the solitude of living on my own with no other energy interrupting my flow. For now, that is my truth. In my now I can't imagine giving up this feeling and independence, but if the universe reveals a man that changes my mind, I will fearlessly follow that yes energy. I will feel my way through each new decision. Will we maintain our own residences so we have alone time? Will I be Polyamorous? I have no idea because it's not time to make those decisions. At this writing I'm still loving the feeling of a monogamous relationship, but I am confident in feeling my inner guidance as that moment presents itself.

- Before this experiment, my longest vacations were three-week trips. Now I'm headed to Greece using a one-way plane ticket and will spend almost four months hopping from one gorgeous destination to another. I'll be away from home for months having fun and being spontaneous.

- I got my first paycheck in this new status as an early retiree. When I opened my banking app on payday to see what the new amount of my direct deposit was . . . I giggled in delight and awe. My new take-home pay being deposited into my account every two weeks moving forward is now double what it was. DOUBLE! Holy shit! I'm literally getting paid double to do nothing, to do whatever I want. To travel, to live my life like a unicorn: a magical, never-ending weekend.

- When I started my experiment a year ago, I was unsure of so many things. Now I am living in such a confident, steady place of knowing. I truly trust myself. I trust myself to tune into this unicorn frequency and therefore expect what a unicorn expects. A unicorn doesn't question or doubt his ability to live in continuous magic. I now ask myself, "How does this conversation, party, trip, business meeting play out for a unicorn?" It plays out beautifully! It plays out in ways that someone who doesn't claim their unicorn status doesn't experience. You can't have what you don't think is possible.

Now I get to wake up and feel my way through what I want to do next. Of the options in front of me, what sounds the most fun? At this editing stage of my book, it has been seventeen months and I'm still pinching myself and feeling such appreciation for where I am.

It was absolutely "fun" to think of each of you with me on my unicorn journey as I applied what I was learning to my life and as I applied this new approach to each moment directly in front of me.

None of this is technically hard. It's simply counterintuitive to why, what, and *how* we've lived so far. *So far!* It's counterintuitive to how we've been taught to accomplish our dreams. It turns out it's not through blood, sweat, and tears, but through playful, lighthearted energy. Turns out, there's nothing *more* intuitive to the core of our being than having F-U-N. It's the number one reason why we came forth. To play. FUN is a path to transformation. Fun is the unicorn frequency.

That is the very best reason to write a book, to share this magical "how" for living.

So play, damn it! You always wanted to. And now you have the best excuse ever: it's the very fount of abundance!

The frequency of fun puts you in the receptive mode and the unicorn frequency *explodes* your level of expectation. Again, you can't manifest or allow beyond what you expect.

Ask yourself these questions:

- Do you love yourself enough to see yourself as a unicorn?
- Are you ready to expect never-ending magic?
- Are you at least willing to try?
- Can you at least start by asking the universe to show you the ways that you are a unicorn?

Ask: "I want to see the magic of me play out in this meeting. I want to see the unicorn essence of me show up in my life so that I have the life experience that allows me to expect even more to show up. Universe, I want you to show me the magic in today. Show me how good I can feel today."

Alignment is the receptive mode. The receptive mode is where all great ideas come from. It's where all the small, next steps come from too.

Now you get to start your own twelve-month experiment of not just fun, but the UNICORN level of fun. It starts with looking for ways to feel good in every moment. When you feel good, when you expect magic, you are tuning to the unicorn frequency.

If I could leave you with knowing and *feeling* one thing, it would be this: you didn't come to be all things to all people. You came to discover, through living, your preferences. To honor the beauty and magic of *you* and what you prefer. To feel *your* enthusiasm for life and *your* enthusiasm for the choices in front of you. You did not come to live someone else's magic. You did not come to feel someone else's thrill. You came to tune to your full self. So, tune to the fullness of you. Tune to *your* passion for *your* life . . . the pure, undiluted UNICORN version of you.

Wherever you find yourself right now is perfect. Don't make yourself wrong. But an attitude of FUN with where you are and an eager expectation for the "more" that is on its way is the path to an abundant, magical, unicorn life.

Remember, no one else has to like the colors in your rainbow. Your colors are between YOU and you, between the divine you and the human you. Those colors are always beautiful. Those unique colors are the fullness of you.

The world is ready for you and your inner unicorn. The world is hungry for all of our inner unicorns.

Now get out into this big, beautiful world today and go poop a rainbow. Maybe even two!

Acknowledgments

MY PERSONAL AND PROFESSIONAL LIFE HAS TAUGHT ME MUCH of what I've written in this book. I am a passionate advocate for self-improvement. I have passionately and happily invested a lot of time and money into my love and curiosity for this inner work. I gratefully acknowledge and honor the teachers that I have studied with: Abraham Hicks, KT Brady, and Liz Hays. My life has been profoundly changed by their guidance and wisdom. Together we have co-created beyond what I once thought was possible. I am forever appreciative, and I am in awe of each of your individual gifts and wisdom. Thank you!

Thank you to Nancy. It was fun to write our books on parallel paths!

A very special thanks to Azul, Heather, Kim, Amanda, Steve, Kaitlin, my editors, and the entire publishing team for your guidance throughout this process.

About the Author

FROM THE VERY BEGINNING, REID has been following his intuition. He was raised by parents with a keen metaphysical outlook on life and who applied this metaphysical viewpoint in their daily experience.

Photo by Curtis Ebl

As an adult, Reid spent his professional career in the corporate world as a group creative director for a global Fortune 500 company.

During the pandemic, a series of events guided him down a fascinating path of new breadcrumbs that introduced him to the world of meditation, reincarnation, and the law of attraction. From this journey Reid discovered that the deliberate practice of simply having fun has been a counterintuitive yet astonishing path to inner alignment and financial abundance. Reid soon left his corporate job and is now an entrepreneur, designer, and life coach. He continues to enjoy travel and following his passions through a wide variety of creative projects.

I would appreciate your feedback on what chapters helped you most and what you would like to see in future books.

If you enjoyed this book and found it helpful, please leave a **review** on Amazon.

Visit me at

THEUNICORNFREQUENCY.COM

where you can sign up for email updates.

Thank you!

Milton Keynes UK
Ingram Content Group UK Ltd.
UKHW010253130324
439347UK00014B/179/J